FINISHING SCHOOL

for School

Women

Women must take charge.
Love with your heart, rule with your mind.
Learn how to manipulate so you won't be manipulated.

ROMAN PLASTICH

FINISHING SCHOOL FOR WOMEN

iUniverse books may be ordered through booksellers or by contacting:

iUniverse LLC
1663 Liberty Drive
Bloomington, IN 47403
www.iuniverse.com
1-800-Authors (1-800-288-4677)

ISBN: 978-1-4917-3164-2 (sc)
ISBN: 978-1-4917-3165-9 (hc)
ISBN: 978-1-4917-3166-6 (e)

Library of Congress Control Number: 2014906573

Printed in the United States of America.

iUniverse rev. date: 08/18/2014

To the women who know they deserve better
and the ones who are manipulated to believe differently.

This book was inspired by Pamela Rizzo.

CONTENTS

Guidelines To Go By

PREFACE

This book is a practical and useful way of responding to and dealing with your relationship challenges. All the stories are true, and they have been shared within a circle of friends with no fear of repercussion. The stories are from people who grew up in a culture of manipulation in which people are led to believe one partner needs the relationship more than the other ... where it is believed that men can get away with everything they want ... where men and women are encouraged to satisfy their own needs before they address their partner's. It's not a survey or a report from experts who have spent years in classrooms analyzing other people's lives. If you want to get the uncensored truth, you cannot rely on putting a microphone in front of a stranger and asking him what happened behind closed doors. They only way to know is to be there.

INTRODUCTION

I have always been fascinated by the way people's perspectives change when things happen to them in their relationships in comparison to how they feel when it happens to their friends. They can be rational, give good advice, and point out the obvious to their friends, but when they find themselves in a relationship with the same challenges, common sense goes out the window. Women are more susceptible to that because of their kinder nature and desire to live "happily ever after."

We've all had broken hearts. Some of us have said, "Never again!" And some have believed it's better to have loved and lost than to never have loved. I belong to the first group, and the men who had an influence on my friends and me were of the same mentality. Here's what we were taught: Being in charge in a relationship is the way to go. There is no such thing as equal partners. It's always better getting things done your way than deciding together. Relationships are about power. If you're not the one in control, the one wearing the pants, she will take over. If you give her a finger, she will take the whole hand. To win in this game you need skills; you need to understand women's weaknesses. If you gain this knowledge, you will be able to manipulate them.

As it is with anything else in life, if you behave a certain way often enough over a long enough period of time and associate with the people who hold the same beliefs, you will get good at it. Many times I've heard, "You should write a book or start a blog." I get this from guys who have had trouble with their ladies. I'm glad I didn't.

It would be a much different book from the one you are reading now. Instead of trying to teach people how to have happy and healthy relationships, it would just teach men how to manipulate even more. Until a few years ago, I didn't know what I didn't know. What is it like to have someone that you want to be with all the time? What is it like to have a partner and a best friend all in one person? I know that, at that time, I would be laughing at these words and swearing that I would never say them, but as I said, I didn't know what I didn't know.

Of course it took a woman to show me the right way of thinking—the right woman for me. There are a lot of good women and good men out there, but the match has to be perfect. The problem is not that there is a one-in-a-million chance that you will run into that person; the problem is that we don't have the skills to connect on that level. Yes, you need chemistry and passion. You cannot fake or teach that. But chemistry and passion are not enough to make it work.

I have been inspired by my girlfriend, Pamela. She took me from that "never again" mind-set to the "better to have loved and lost than never loved again" mind-set. She took me from "love is for teenagers who don't know any better" to "you're never too old to fall in love." I hope this book helps millions of couples to wake up the love that they had for each other in the beginning of their relationships and helps millions of singles to create their own forever-and-ever relationships. Even if I get only one e-mail saying, "Thanks, your book helped me find what I was looking for," it will be worth the effort. If you knew me and what a skeptic I have always been, you would have no doubt that my advice can work for you. I wish all of you will be able to find what I have.

UNDERSTANDING YOURSELF AND WHAT YOU ARE LOOKING FOR

CHAPTER 1

I Woke Up Dreaming Black and White

I never noticed whether we dream in colors or just black and white until the morning after I lost Pamela. I just had the most vivid dream. I don't remember the dream; all I remember is that it was so black and white. I don't even know what the message of that may be; I just know it really left an impression on me. That was the very beginning of this book. My emotions, thoughts, and outlooks on certain things started to become so clear to me, just like my black-and-white dream. I started to understand the rationale behind the outlook Pamela had on relationships. She used to say that she would like to open a finishing school for women. Women need to be shown how to demand the respect and love they want and deserve from a man … how to set the standards by which a man should treat them. Too many women have been doormats in their relationships. Their kindness has been abused by their significant others. Women have suffered throughout history at the hands of men without a chance of a change or the possibility of getting out of such relationships. Even in this day and age, many women stay in relationships in which they are miserable rather than leave. I believe that is because women are relationship oriented. They will try for a long time to make it work. Despite all that, sometimes they will come to a point of no return. More and more divorces today are initiated by women who feel they have been constantly giving and giving and receiving nothing in return. They take care of the home, the husband, the kids, and everybody else's needs and get little in return. One day they just reach a point of saturation, and they are gone. That's when men find themselves thinking, *What happened?* Often relationships break down because women simply cannot relay their messages to men in a way they can understand.

Ladies, I did not write this book to show you how to leave your man or how to stay in an unhappy marriage. I wrote this book to show you how to find the right man for you, how to show him what you have to give, and how to show him what you expect in return. True relationships should not be power struggles; rather, they should be partnerships between two equal, loving, and respectful partners.

Yes, I know you agree. You've heard it all before, and it's easier said than done. But as long as you are ready to give it a shot and carry on a relationship in a way a man can understand you, it's very possible. Men will adapt; we will make changes. We will start doing things for you just to hear you say, "I Love You. Thank you. You're my hero. I'm so lucky." Right now, many men will do things for their women only when they really have to, when they are constantly nagged, or in order to collect "points" that they can use later when they want to do something without their partners, like going golfing or fishing or engaging in any other hobby. Men have a hard time experiencing or even believing in the kind of relationship in which we do things just for love—especially those we call alpha males, who see too much, experience too much, and have been womanizers all their lives.

These alpha men, too, will get married. They will love their wives the best way they know how, but they will hardly stay interested in that one woman after she offers no challenge and never rewards his ego. These men know how to do little things—romantic gestures, moments of sweetness—that will earn them points they can trade in for their other interests. But that crazy love they felt for you in the beginning will not stay with them just because they said, "I do." At first they may do nice things just to put a smile on your face, but that behavior will fade away unless you know how to demand it from them, and I'm not talking about communicating with him verbally. That's what you call it; we call it nagging.

My father told me two things about relationships: First, "Never run after a bus or a woman, because there will always be another bus and another woman." That one is pretty self-explanatory. Second, "Make sure your woman loves you a little bit more than you love her." There you go. How can you go wrong with that? While you girls are dreaming about your perfect wedding, we are learning a different song. The one who loves more has more to lose. The one who loves more will sacrifice more. The one who loves more will always make sure to please you, to put your needs before hers, to make sure you are happy even if you don't give half as much back. What lovely advice. Well, my father didn't know better, and neither did I. I was a pretty good son in that regard. All you need to do is seem to pay attention to her, remember a few little things from time to time that she has said, and she will think you have been listening. Make small romantic gestures, and they will mean the world to her. It's called "collecting points." Well, that was before the Pamela era.

Of course I would have done the same thing to her if she'd let me. On our second date I told her jokingly, "You love me. You just don't know it yet." She laughed and said, "You and a hundred others." Now that's an alpha female. There were no hundred others, but her confidence in the fact that, if I wasn't there, a hundred others were ready to take my place showed me what kind of woman she was. She would not sit at home and cry over me if it didn't work out after six months. She would move on. This is not the sort of woman that many men can please and keep around. It takes a real man to keep her interested, and of course I thought I was that man. Every man wants to be that man. We don't want a woman any man can have, just like you don't want a man no other woman wants.

So she turned me from a womanizer to a woman lover. The more I understood how much women can hurt, how devoted they can be, how they can put themselves unconditionally in the shadow for someone they love, the more I could appreciate really good relationships and really enjoy that kind of love. The strength a woman has and the pain she is willing to go through when she is in love makes a man feel special if he understands what she is willing to do for him. When a woman loves, she does not think about "upgrading" as many men often do after they achieve success in life. Women will never say it's okay to look as long as you don't touch, as men do. They don't need recognition from other men that they've still "got it." A woman's family circuit is her whole world. Forever and ever is not a sales pitch; it's the standard women live by. Women are better people than we are, but we will adapt. We can learn to be the men you deserve, but we can't do it on our own. We need to be taught, and to be taught in a language we understand. Men are capable of being the men you want them to be, but you must teach them how. We want to be your heroes. We want to be the special ones in your lives, and we will fulfill your requirements. Each of us wants that special woman on our arm that no other man can have.

I hope couples benefit from this book. I hope you find your hero, because life is about experience, and a truly loving relationship is an experience we should all have in our lives. In this book you can see that this sort of relationship can be achieved at any stage of your life. It doesn't matter if you just started a relationship or if you've been married for twenty years. As long as you haven't reached that point of no return where you've had enough, there is a chance you can wake up your love. Perhaps you are with a new love. Perhaps you are waking up an old love with your spouse and you've even forgotten the reasons you married. It's up to you. You can find it, but you will have to do the work.

CHAPTER 2

Who Are You?

The most important information you must have before you search for a fulfilling relationship with someone who is right for you is basic: you must know what you want. It sounds simple, and of course it makes sense. We all know what we want. Well, not really. Most of us know what we don't want, but that is not enough. Knowing what we don't like or don't want is not that important. Knowing what we do want is the key.

What you want is much more than just the opposite of what you don't want. You can say, "I don't want anyone who doesn't put family first. I don't want someone who is not a good provider. I don't want someone who is not a good husband or father. I don't want a man who still thinks that he should be going out with his boys and keeps all his hobbies from his single days. I don't want a man who wants to be the boss and not an equal partner." Well, you can get all that in a man and still not be happy.

Your man can say, "I work hard. I'm a good provider. I don't go out with the boys drinking and gambling. I don't chase other women. I come home, I play with the kids, and I take them to their sports events. I do anything around the house I can do. I am a good husband and father." And that may all be true—not a word of it a lie. Now when you talk about that same man, you may say, "Yes he is a good provider. He works hard. He takes care of his family, but …" Now comes the part when you talk about what you really want—what you personally and emotionally need from him to be happy. "But we never do anything together, just the two of us. We don't connect. He is not affectionate with me. There are no small gestures of kindness. He doesn't say thank you or tell me he loves me. He never shows me that he's happy to be with me. His gifts to me are always something for the house, never something romantic just for me. If there were no kids or bills, we would have nothing to talk about; we would have no reason to stay together."

A couple I know, Bill and Mary, are just like that. Bill is a great provider. He works really hard. He comes home and takes the boys to sports events every night of the week. They have four boys, and he's never free—always busy, either with work or kids. A few of us used to play ball together, and one night we decided we should set a date to get together for drinks one evening. Six months later it still hasn't happened. Bill never has the time. Everything is about the kids, bills, and the house. Bill and Mary have never taken a trip together. She has taken the boys to the old country; he stayed home and worked. Once a year he takes a long weekend to go fishing. So after eighteen years of marriage, they haven't done anything together or for each other. She complains that he is never romantic; there is never a moment that is just the two of them. They have lost that connection, the feeling of belonging to each other. They just go through the routine day after day. She complains he never says, "I love you." He says, "I told you I loved you when I married you. If anything changes, you will be the first to know." She says, "When he's home, he's either working around the house or watching TV." He says, "Things need to get done, and even a donkey needs to sit down sometimes." She says, "He doesn't need to work so much. We can enjoy a little bit now." He says, "Do you know how much college costs? Do you think we can retire on a government pension?"

They are both good people, but Bill is too much about providing and taking care of the physical needs of his family. At the same time, he doesn't understand that Mary needs to feel loved, cherished, and appreciated. She needs that kind of connection with her husband more than she needs the physical security he provides. She would be much happier with more of "us" … more of an emotional satisfaction than extra money for security for her life. There are women who are fine with that kind of life, but only those who are fine with it should agree to it. Nobody is right or wrong here, but the question is, are they right for each other?

So if you know only what you *don't* want, that doesn't mean you will get what you *do* want, so you'd better be clear about what kind of a life and what kind of a man you are looking for. The most important thing in finding that perfect guy is knowing what you want first. It's not just about good and bad, right and wrong. It's about how your personalities match. It's been said that opposites attract. It may be fun in the beginning—you're both experiencing new things, trying out new things that you never did before. Sooner or later, these experiences and emotions won't be new anymore. You will have less fun doing them over and over. Maybe your partner will still enjoy them, but you will start to compromise. Pretty soon there will be too many things that you do separately, or one of you will be compromising all the time. You have to know what you like, what your values in life are, and what is important to you. We are all somewhat products of our environments—how we were raised, how our fathers and mothers treated one another. We all observed the dynamics of men and women in general—friends and relatives—all around us as we were growing up. What we saw may not have been necessarily good or bad, just different.

The smallest things can create tension. If you have an argument, you might have been taught never to go to bed angry, and he might have been taught to sleep on it because after rest the brain is more rational. Nobody is right or wrong here, but two different approaches can cause further disagreements. That is a small example. When it comes to making extra money or going to the kids' soccer game, having a bigger house or having more time with the kids, sharing and helping each other or dividing chores—these situations can really create a divide between partners. Personality plays a big part too—active adventurer compared to couch potato, nature lover compared to big-city lover. Clashes in personalities can be enough to make a couple miserable after many years of compromising and giving in. Yes, you may go through rough times sometimes, but don't you think you would choose to be with someone because you are happier with that person in your life than you would be on your own? Women have a right to have their needs fulfilled, to receive affection from a man, to receive as much love as they give.

Life shouldn't be just going to a job, coming home, cooking, cleaning, watching TV, and going to bed (repeat and repeat and repeat day after day). Even when the kids are grown up and out of the house, women put up with this sort of existence because they think that's all there is in life. Maybe they are afraid to be alone or they're in love with the concept of marriage and not really with the man they are married to. And why would they be in love with him? They're more of a servant than a partner.

You can change your situation at any time if you speak the language men understand, but better yet, don't let it come to that. Pick the right man for you. You will go through hard times in life, but they shouldn't be because of your choice of partner. He should be there in the capacity you need him to be, and he will be if you show him how. And, yes, you will have to remind him from time to time. We don't think the way you do, but we love to be praised by you. So learn how to help your man fulfill your needs and stay connected with him. It's easier said than done, but at least give yourself a chance. Figure out what you want—what kind of man you want—and I will show you in this book how to figure out if he is the one ... the one who will reach your standards and fulfill your needs.

A good way to decide upon the type of relationship you would like to have (or would like to avoid) is to observe other people around you. Your family and your friends are the ones you already know a lot about. How do these men treat their partners? What do the women like, and what do they complain about? Again, some of them are stuck in their routines, some of them are in love with the concept of a relationship, and some of them just don't want to be alone. All that is fine, and it's their right to decide what they are ready to put up with or what is most important to them in their relationships. Just don't let them convince you that's all there is. Don't let them tell you that you are a dreamer ... that you will see when you get married how things change. That is their reality; it doesn't have to be yours. Those women don't know how to get help, respect, or love from their men because they don't know how to express their requirements and expectations to their men. They make their choices and compromises, but they also have their own priorities, and maybe they are fine with them. You haven't walked in their shoes, so don't judge them, but also don't blindly believe their ideas.

I was blown away by something my distant cousin told me a while ago. She was an attractive, vibrant woman who was a spirited supporter of women's rights. Well, that's how she looked to me. She got married pretty young, and probably did it to get away from her controlling father—one of those fathers who demand that girls to be old fashioned, quiet, and pretty. So she ended up marrying a bad boy, a tough guy. Well the tough guy had no ambitions. He would go to work, watch TV, and play video games. He didn't drink, he didn't gamble, and didn't chase women. He didn't do anything else, for that matter, with or without her. She had to be responsible for anything that had to be done—organizing, making calls, doing paper work, planning and overseeing renovations. He had no drive for anything. All he was good at was guarding his place on the couch. One day she said to me, "You know, if he had some life in him—if he wanted to do something, go on vacations, reach for some goals, just live life and experience life—I wouldn't even care if he cheated on me." I looked at her with my mouth wide open. Then she said, "Well, I probably wouldn't even find out anyway, but at least I wouldn't be sitting in this house waiting to die."

Now, I'm not telling you that's okay. I'm just telling you, here is a vibrant young woman full of life. She wants to live but cannot because of the partner she picked. She won't fulfill her dreams on her own because she doesn't think it's right for a married woman to do things alone as if she were single. So she just lets her life go by. Pride is not a priority to her. Her husband's fidelity was not the most important thing to her—or maybe she wanted a reason for a divorce. I didn't ask. I was surprised, but I understood that, in her eyes, anything would be better than what she had. Luckily for my cousin, her husband left her to look for a pot of gold at the end of the rainbow. She remarried a few years later to a very nice guy who also loves his couch and doesn't want to do much either. Why do we seem to follow the same patterns?

A couple of years ago I asked her, "What would you do if you won twenty million dollars?" She said, "I would travel." I said, "Okay, for the first couple of years. But after that you would go on trips three or four times a year. What would you do between trips? You would have to do something." Here's the surprise answer she gave me: "I don't know." I said, "You don't know what you want?" She said, "No, I don't know, but I would figure something out." I said, "Yeah, sure you would."

So you'd better know what you want. You'd better know what kind of man you want. Do you want to stay home, make wine, grow a garden, and host Tupperware parties? Or do you want something else?

It's about you. Who will complement you? Whom will you complement? Now don't go looking for that perfect relationship— the perfect couple you want to look up to around the holidays. Times like Christmas, when everyone is happy, jolly, and well fed are not good indications of real situations. Pick Wednesday, laundry day, or any other "regular" day. Have drinks with your girlfriends. Talk about things and get them to open up. Ask them what they would change if they could go back ten years. Now, if they have kids, they might say nothing because they love their kids. But ask what would they like more of from their husbands—or even less of. What are they missing emotionally or physically or any other form? Don't let them tell you a good relationship cannot be achieved. Don't let them tell you all the daily responsibilities stand in the way. Ask them, if the day-to-day problems were magically taken care of, what would they like more of out of life? You will find similar things from many women. It's always about the time—time for herself, time alone with her husband, more affection from him, more understanding and connecting.

Now you can talk about your expectations—how you want your life to be, what kind of marriage you want, what kind of man you want. Your friends will probably call you a dreamer. They will say that's what they wanted too. They'll say that life doesn't work that way; life always throws you a surprise. They'll always blame situations or circumstances rather than taking responsibility and taking action to change things. It's always about money, taking care of kids, husbands who don't help, not enough time in the day for everything. Well, let's see.

How much money does it take for your husband to bring you flowers twice a month for no reason at all except to say I love you and I appreciate all you do? For $4.99 he could pick up a bouquet in the grocery store. It doesn't have to be long-stemmed roses for $50. How much does it cost to pick up dinner from the little bakery around the corner once a week? Maybe $20? And that will give you two extra hours because you won't have to cook or clean up. Kids can have prepackaged lunches from the supermarket once a week for school; they won't die from it. Now you have a free evening. You're not tired. Wear something nice that he likes, open a bottle of wine, play some music, maybe from the old days when you were young and dating. Just enjoy each other. Fall asleep on the couch, watch a movie, make love. There's really nothing stopping you from doing that.

When there is no desire to make even a little effort, it is always easy to come up with a hundred excuses why you cannot have this sort of "fun." It's not the responsibilities, it's not kids, it's not bills. It's the partner you are with—the partner who's not worth the effort. It is a partner you are disconnected from. Or maybe you are not worth the effort for him.

Your friends will not be able to give you constructive answers as to why a successful relationship cannot be maintained. They will all keep telling you, "You will see when you get married." And you will. You will get what you demand, so set the way you expect to be treated and you will get exactly that.

In the Bahamas my girlfriend and I were walking through the Atlantis Hotel. An older man in his sixties approached us and gave us a compliment. He said he thought we looked like a nice couple, and he told my girlfriend, Pamela, "You are the most beautiful woman I have seen on this island." (And she is stunning!) He paused a little bit, and my girl said, "Thank you so much. You are so sweet." And then he said, "Only until tomorrow. My wife of thirty-two years is coming tomorrow. She couldn't come with me, but she is coming tomorrow, and I can't wait to see her." Of course my girlfriend was so touched, she started to cry, and when she saw his wife the next day, she had to meet her. Pamela told the man's wife about her husband and wished them all the best. Now do you think life never threw challenges their way? Do you think they never had any money problems? Do you think their kids raised themselves from the day they were born and everything was smooth sailing for them? No, each of them had simply found the right person to share life with.

The most important decision in your life is choosing your partner, so set your requirements. Know what you want and choose wisely. Don't leave it to chance and just hope for the best.

I created this quiz to help you establish and recognize your needs in a relationship. Questions like this do not usually come up ahead of time; rather, they surprise us all when a particular situation occurs. It's better to know the answers before the questions can surprise us. These issues can create a real strain between you and your partner, because his priorities and understanding of relationships and family may be totally different from yours. What is the role you expect your man to play when it comes to financial support, raising children, keeping up with family traditions and culture and all-around involvement in your family unit? This quiz does not have a points system. It's not for me to evaluate your needs or for you to try to get the most favorable view of yourself. The only purpose is to help you discover what priorities you are looking for in a man. This should help you be more capable of choosing the right man for you.

Quiz

1. Your man will:

    a. Make significantly more money than you.
    b. Make about the same as you.
    c. Be employed and ambitious.
    d. This consideration doesn't matter.

2. In your marriage:

    a. Your husband makes the money and you are a stay-at-home mom.
    b. You both work; he does the man's chores and you do the woman's.
    c. You both work and share chores to the best of your abilities.
    d. You make all the money and he stays home.

3. What would you rather have?

    a. An extra vacation (trip with the family).
    b. House renovations or a new car.
    c. $1,000 extra per week (with your husband working long hours).
    d. Your husband coming home for the kids' sports and games.

4. You expect from your husband to:

    a.   Show you kindness and appreciation daily.

    b.   Show you kindness and appreciation from time to time.

    c.   Show kindness and appreciation by actions (chores/flowers) not words.

    d.   Showing kindness and appreciation by doing things the way you want them to be done.

5. You wish to spend your vacation:

    a.   At a cottage or camping with the family.

    b.   On an all-inclusive trip with the family.

    c.   on separate but equal vacations without the family

6. Your free time and hobbies are:

    a.   Very important to you.

    b.   Something you will do if there is time.

    c.   Put on hold indefinitely.

7. Your feelings about his free time and hobbies:

    a.   He should put them on hold indefinitely.

    b.   He can keep them all and you will manage.

    c.   They are important but must be properly scheduled.

8. Your family and traditions compared to his are:

    a.   More important.

    b.   Just as important and have to be balanced.

    c.   You will adopt his.

9. The man you would pick is:

    a. Rich, unavailable, and busy.
    b. Poor but has great character.
    c. Ugly and 100 percent family oriented.
    d. Attractive and challenging.
    e. Average in everything.

CHAPTER 3

We Are Wired Differently

Throughout this book I will repeat a few ideas that are important but difficult to grasp. It is a simple fact that men rationalize things differently from the way women rationalizes things. Our focus is unique, and our scale of importance is upside down compared to yours. The hard-wired differences between the sexes have to be accepted as given before you can move forward and get what you want. First I will talk about a man's needs. Now the key word is *need*—not a hobby, not a pastime, and not entertainment.

A Man's Needs:
- Sex
- To provide
- To protect

A Woman's Needs
- To nurture (Motherhood)
- To "nest"
- To experience a relationship and an emotional connection

Let's examine these ideas through the needs of men:

Sex: Men's need for sex is just a strong as a woman's need to be a mother. First let's get something out of the way. Your needs are more noble and of higher moral standing. Your values in life are more spiritual, emotional, kind, and caring. That's great. We men are more like primates running through the jungle looking to procreate, compete with each other, and impose our will over others. Now that we have that out of the way and you accept it, let's see how can you get us out of the jungle.

So, need number one is sex. Now why is it like that? I don't know, and I don't care. I didn't start any of it, and you shouldn't care either why it's that way. But you have to accept it. Maybe we over compensate. Maybe we are always "in the mood" because you're not, so any time you are ready we'd better be too. If we were moody like you, this species would cease to exist. So making my point short, we need sex, and if we don't get it in one place we will get it somewhere else. You may think your man is different, or you may think you know some men who are. That is a comforting thought, but let me assure you that all the women who have caught their husbands cheating were thinking the same thing. Remember this: most likely you will be the last one to find out if your husband is cheating, and it's not because nobody cares about you. It's quite the opposite; no one wants to be the one to deliver that news to you. Nobody wants to watch you hurt. In fact, this is one of the reasons that most women who are cheated on never find out. Another fact is that men put a lot of effort to hide something they may be ashamed of or something that could bring negative consequences to them. So, please, after understanding all this, you owe it to yourself to know that your husband really isn't different. It's not that you just want to believe he's different. Remember, just because he's your husband, he isn't different from the rest. You have to accept that. We may put up with you for a while, but sooner or later the number-one need will be taken care of by you or someone else. Accept it. It is the truth, and it is your man too. There is no how; there is no why. Just accept it.

To provide: For thousands of years, men have been the providers—and sole providers until the last fifty or sixty years or so. Even though women also worked the fields, gathered wood and food and so on, the perception was that a man is the one who brings home the bacon. That's what we do.

We make sure that family needs are met (at least decent men do, and there are still plenty of them around). From the time we were hunters then farmers then factory workers we have provided for our families. We go out, face the challenges of the world, and bring home the bacon. We provide essential physical life needs the best we can. We can't get down, can't get discouraged, and can't cry over injustices done to us. We are trained to shake those off—be a man and take care of things. We don't come home and ask you, "What are we going to do?" We think more along the lines of, "What am *I* going to do? This is on me. It's my responsibility to provide for this family. I have to find the solution." We don't need to share; we need to take care of situations. We don't need help. We don't like reading instructions or asking for directions, never mind asking for help for something that is an essential part of our existence. That's why we have a hard time talking and sharing our feelings. We talk to find a solution to a problem, not to share our problems with someone so we can feel that someone cares. We are not built to be sensitive, romantic, or emotional. We see these attributes as weaknesses, and they handicap us in the role we have to play to be good providers. Yes, I know times have changed from what they were a hundred years ago, but it also takes time for change to happen. Something we did for thousands of years—something that is part of our DNA—doesn't just change in fifty years, especially not on its own. You will have to help. You will have to help us understand that, even though our role has changed, we are still the men that you rely on and believe in. You still feel confident in our ability to give the family what it needs.

However those needs have changed, it's still as important as it was a thousand years ago for us to provide them. You don't need him to go out and hunt down your next meal, but you do need him to do something else pertinent to the times we live in. We don't know what that is; you do. You know what you need from your men.

Now at the same time men were providers, women made the home. They created a place where all the troubles go away—a sanctuary for the man and children. I don't need to mention the importance of women's jobs; you know it, and so do we. We are not trained or rewired yet to know how to express our appreciation in the way you would like us to, and we need some guidance from you. Our jobs outside of the family are not as tough as they used to be, so we can help you with yours, but we will not volunteer. If you want to do everything by yourself, and you think you're better at it anyway, we won't interrupt you.

To protect: Even though in this day and age there is less need for a man to provide protection than ever before, we still feel it's on us if anything goes wrong. We want to know that you feel that we are capable of protecting if it is necessary. The opportunity is rare, but men know that if anybody or anything ever tried to hurt his family, he would stand in front of it: a raging storm, a man with a gun, a pack of wolves. No matter what, he would die first trying to protect.

We feel this way as long as our needs are met and we feel that, as a man in the household, we can evolve. Our role can change as long as whatever we do now still feels like providing for the good of the family. We will be okay with the change. We can include you and talk to you about our problems, but you have to show confidence that we will take care of it. We can show weakness and emotion to you as long as you don't take out our "fangs."

So you have to show full confidence in your man. Don't doubt him or try to do things for him; that will make him feel less of a man. Of course we like the reward at the end of the day. So accepting how we process the world and our role in it will help you to get what you want from your man. If you're unhappy and you want to share that emotion with your partner, he feels he's responsible for your unhappiness. You might just want someone just to listen, but we feel you want us to fix it. We want to make you feel happy and proud of us; we want to be your hero. That is what we do ... what makes us what we are.

Everything a man does is influenced by one of these needs, and as long as those needs are met, he will be open to fulfilling your needs. Now there are always exceptions to the rules. There are relationships that exist on a totally different understanding of what each other's roles are. In this book I'm talking about the vast majority of the relationships in today's world, which are based on the same principles and same dynamics between men and women that relationships have been based on for many years.

Chapter 4

How to Meet a Man

Now this is the most ridiculous question in the whole concept of relationships. Don't you find it absurd that men are always looking to meet a woman, and women don't know how to meet men? Men are hunters. They are expected to approach and make first contact, and they are aware of it and eager to do so. We are always open to meet a woman no matter where we are. It can be at work, at a bar, at a coffee shop, or at a grocery store. Men will always notice a woman and think about how they could meet her. Yes, I know you are looking to meet a good man—the right man for you—but in order to do that you have to go through the process of actually meeting people before you can know if there is a chance of one of them being "the one." He might walk by you a million times, but if the first contact is not made, you will never know if he's the one.

First, let me explain the processes that go through a man's mind once he notices you—the thought process of a good man and the thought process of the man that you want to avoid. We start with the notion that you women are difficult. If it was up to us, it would be very simple: "Hi. How are you? I find you very attractive. I'd like to take you on a date or for coffee and see what happens." Well, that doesn't work with you ladies too well. Most women who are approached like that in a coffee shop or grocery store would say,

"No, thank you." We don't know why, and I'm not sure if you do. Yes, he could be a nutcase or a rapist or a lunatic, but someone you meet in a dark bar could be "the one" also. Some women would say, "What am I? This is all the effort I get? Just like that? It's easy, so I should just go for it?" Some will say, "He has to do better than that. He needs to chase me." Others may say, "I don't know who meets like that. It sounds weird." So men throw that idea out the window.

Next if you're a somewhat attractive woman, we figure you get hit on all the time, so we feel we have to come up with something original … something that will separate us from the rest and catch your attention. See, we don't realize that you may not be approached all the time because many guys will be discouraged just by that sort of thinking.

Of course, there are other kinds of men—"the vultures" who realize it's all in the numbers: the more women you approach, sooner or later you get a winner. Let's just stay with the decent men for now. Decent guys are more insecure and more affected by rejection. It brings down their self-esteem. They look for signs from you to approach. They need an opening—maybe a look or a smile … something to give them courage to risk embarrassment or rejection. Remember, we are driven by our egos, we are goal oriented, and we are hunters. In the wild, lions and cheetahs are not going to take a run at something that is too far away … something they don't think they can catch. They wait until they are surer of success. In the same way, men need a smile or a look or any sign from you. We need to feel comfortable about our chance of success. People say it doesn't matter if you fall; all that matters is that you get up and try again. That's great advice to give to others, but it can be difficult to apply it to yourself. So picture a guy standing in a bar. He sees you there. What thoughts are going through his mind? The first thought is that he wants to approach you. He wants to meet you. And of course he wants to sleep with you. He's attracted to you, and that's a given as long as it's not the only thing he wants from you.

For the ones who *only* want to sleep with you, it's all about the numbers as I have already said. That kind of a guy will scan the bar for a while. You might see him around, and then he'll disappear. He evaluates the scene. He knows that plan A might not work, so he needs a plan B and a plan C. He will find three or four suitable candidates and make sure he approaches the one who is off to the side first. He doesn't want the other ones to see him approaching someone else before he approaches them. Nobody wants to be the second choice or third or who knows which. It's the same thing with the guy who comes to the bar an hour before closing. Do you think he was sitting at home till now and just came out? No, he was somewhere else, probably in a different bar, and he had no luck there. This is his last stop to get lucky. Nothing is a 100 percent rule, but most of the time that is the scenario. He will approach you fast because there is not much time left. He will give you a lot of compliments or try to impress you by his accomplishments or the toys he has. He will not engage in any meaningful conversation. He is not here to get to know you, just to get you. He wants to find out fast if there's going to be any action. If there isn't, he will still have time to move on.

Now there is the guy who will approach you early on in the evening, but he can't stay around all night long. If he really likes you, he will ask for your number quite early in the conversation. He may be ready to work on you—go on a date with you—but he knows nothing is going to happen that night, and he wants something right now. If you hit it off well and he has to leave early but wants your number, he is either married or he likes you but needs something for the night and is going to check out another bar. He can't go hitting on someone else in this bar right in front of you, and the night is still young, so there's time for him to get lucky. So, if you like him (And who knows? Maybe that is not what he's doing.), you ask for his number and you'll see. The night is still young for you too. Who knows whom you'll meet by the end of it? Maybe someone who has time for you and only you … maybe a good guy.

So let's get back to the good guy and how he thinks. As I said, he sees you standing there. He knows there are other people checking you out. Now he has to go across the room and come to you, start talking to you, risk the rejection, and then do the "walk of shame" to his place in the corner of the bar if you do, indeed, reject him. Believe me, to him it feels as if everyone in the bar is watching what happens. It's a very long walk back. After he does it a few times, he'll ask himself why he even bothers, and the next time he won't unless he gets a little sign of insurance that you might like him too. So you need to give him the green light; give him a signal that it's okay to approach. It doesn't mean that he will score; it doesn't mean anything except "Let's talk and see what happens." At least he will feel he will be able to stand there and talk to you for a few minutes and not look like a reject.

So, ladies, if you want a decent man you will have to help out a little bit. If you make it too hard for him to approach you, only the guys who "work the numbers" will come over. They will be the only ones with enough guts, because they know sooner or later they will get lucky. Afterward it will be everyone's fault but yours, and every man will be an ass in your eyes.

But remember, not every man is an ass; it's just the ones who approach you … the ones that you attract. You have to realize that you have some responsibility regarding what kind of man you will attract. The way you behave, the way you dress, and how you interact with men will have a lot to do with the kind of men who approach you. If you put on a sleazy dress (not sexy with class—I mean sleazy) and go grind with your girlfriends on the dance floor, what do you think the guy approaching you is thinking? I bet it's not, *I can't wait for my mother to meet her.*

Yes, ladies, you have the power. It's time to learn how to use it. The first thing is eye contact, and I don't mean a glance across the room. Look at him for a couple of seconds, and smile. Yes, maybe you'll have to do it two or three times before he feels good about approaching you. If you're in a group of girls, it's more difficult for him, so you should excuse yourself at some point. Be the first to leave the dance floor and sit down. Go to the washroom; he will probably be standing somewhere on your route back to your seat when you return. Guys are also always around the bar hoping a girl will come stand beside him to order a drink. That makes it easy for him to say, "Hi. How are you?" He can introduce himself and not have to do the walk of shame. If he offers you a drink, say, "No thank you." But let him know that you would like one in an hour or so (if you're interested). Tell him you are with your girlfriend and you don't want to leave her alone, so he should give you a little time with her. Afterward, he's welcome to join you guys. Now you will see what he's going to do for that next hour. Is he going to be hitting on someone else? Does he have a plan B or C? Or is he waiting for that hour to go by? It also makes you look better in his eyes. You're not interested in getting free drinks. You can't be bought or impressed easily. You're here with your friend open to possibility but not looking for a quick hookup.

Now, as I said, men will also stand on the route to and from the women's washroom. All of you have to go there at some point. It's crowded. You'll have to squeeze by, and it's a great opportunity for guys to say something. That's the easy way for him to break the ice and meet you, but you still have to be accessible. If he invites you for a drink, do the same thing and see what he's doing there. Is he working on a plan B or C or focusing on you?

We'll talk later about the things that you do or say when you meet a guy, and how to find out what he's about. You have to remember that you have all the power; you need to control the conversation, get him out of his comfort zone, and see how he reacts. If he's a sleaze ball, he's not going to tell you. If he did, he would never get lucky. He has his routine: he'll keep the conversation light, try to get you to talk all the time, and reveal as little as possible about himself unless it's something to impress you.

Now meeting a guy while pursuing everyday life activities is pretty much the same. We guys still need that opening. It's also more acceptable for you to make the first contact. First thing you have to do is to stop going through your days like guys watching sports.

I'm sure you've seen guys watching games on TV—maybe your ex-boyfriend, your friends, your father. They totally tune everything else out. Unless you walk right in front of the TV, they won't even notice you. They'll just yell for you to move. Well that's exactly how you women are; you walk through the day not noticing anyone around you. You will sit in a coffee shop reading your book. George Clooney himself could walk in, and you would not see him. You buy groceries like you're solving world peace—as if nothing is more important than if the cantaloupes are ripe. What about if you go shopping, what happens then? How many times have you gone into a store to buy one thing and also ended up buying something else because it was a great deal? You go to buy jeans and end up coming out with a T-shirt or a sweater or shoes as well. How did you ever see the bargain if you only looked for the jeans? Why did you look around to see if there was anything else? How did you even notice it? Well I guess you must have looked around. You were interested to see if there was something else you liked. What a crazy concept. Who would ever think of that? You don't have to try on everything you look at, but you have to look to find a good deal … to find something you like. It's easy to say to the guy in the coffee shop, "This line seems to be longer every time I come here." or "This is a good business to have. They're always busy." Mention that you come here, let's say, every day or every Tuesday at this time and it's always crazy. Same thing at the grocery store or anywhere else. A guy will remember that information; he will be there next Tuesday at the same time. How do I know? Let's see, you find great shoes in the store, and the salesman tells you that they are going on sale next Saturday and they have a lot of them in stock. I bet you will remember. So the second time the guy sees you it's easy for him to say hi; it's easy to start the small talk. He feels very comfortable. Remember the whole world is like a mall. Open your eyes. Be approachable. You will find some good deals wherever you go, and just like shopping you're the one who decides if you're just looking, ready to try something on, or ready to take something home for keeps.

CREATING AN ENVIRONMENT FOR THE RIGHT MAN

CHAPTER 5

Online Dating

Now when it comes to online dating, it's a little more difficult to figure out which candidates you should give a chance to contact you. In face-to-face encounters, it's easier for a woman to determine if she's interested or not. When you're in the presence of someone, you can feel if there's chemistry; you can tell if there's any physical attraction. On Internet dating sites, you never know how old that picture is. You don't hear a voice, and you cannot look into a person's eyes—the windows to the soul as many would say. On the other hand, you will be approached by more men—or should I say contacted by— and you will not be stuck with someone boring you for hours. You will not have to feel rude by saying you're not interested. You can just delete or block the guy. For a man, online dating is God's gift. There's no feeling of rejection—at least not a direct one—and you ladies know how to give a guy that ugly look when you don't want to be bothered. There's no walk of shame for him with a hundred eyes watching him, everyone wondering how many times he's struck out. Online contact also gives a man a chance to think about what to say. He's read your profile. You have mentioned the things you like or dislike, so he has some guidelines about how to interact with you. He has time to think about you and prepare what to write. In direct contact, whatever he says is "out there"; he can't take it back.

Online he has a chance to read it back to himself, see how it sounds, and correct it if necessary.

Now many men don't know how to write their profiles, and they really don't want to put all their information out there for everyone to see. He doesn't want his buddies to read that he likes long walks on the beach, a glass of wine by a fire, watching romantic movies. He figures he can tell that to a woman once he makes contact with her, so don't get discouraged by the profile with few details. So when a man contacts you, naturally you go to his profile to see what he's about. You look for some signs, some hints, to help you decide whether you should respond or not. You look for something to tell you if this is a man you would want.

Now keep in mind that we don't know how to write these profiles, and we find it a pain in the ass to do so. Many men just put down a little bit of information about themselves and figure, if they fit in your profile, you will contact them and that's fine. If his profile isn't really full of details, it doesn't have to be anything bad. The important part is, when you make contact, you should ask for all those details: What kind of women does he like? What does he expect from you? You probably already have a lot of information in your profile, so there is no need to talk about you. You should remain a little mysterious. Don't give him any more guidelines to go by than he already has. Also, don't let him generalize. He can say, "I can clean up nice for a night on the town, but also like to stay home, relaxing by the fire with a glass of wine." Yes, that sounds nice, and we can all do that, but which activity is more prominent in his life? Don't be afraid to ask. You need to know. As I said before, we don't know how to write these profiles, and we don't want the whole world to see that we enjoy cuddling up by the fire. And that's okay. But once the contact is made, you should ask for all that information. See how he spends his vacation and with whom. How does he spend his free time? Get all of his interests out there and see if they're compatible with yours.

Now if a man wants to meet you just for coffee or a walk or anything that you're not tied down for two or three hours like a fancy dinner, that is a good thing. He wants to see if there is chemistry, if you two will click. He doesn't want to waste his time. If you don't click, it doesn't mean you're not good enough; it just means you just don't suit him. He doesn't want to waste your time. He doesn't need to get you somewhere where you are more or less trapped and he has more time to impress you and convince you to go on a second date. No, he just wants to meet you and see how you two get along. Can something develop here? Is there a physical attraction? Were you truthful on your profile?

You don't want to waste your time responding to all the e-mails you get; you want to weed out the bad ones and focus on the ones that interest you … the ones you think you might be compatible with and have a chance at more than just a couple of dates with. So I'm going to give you some guidelines from a man's perspective of online dating. It's like everything else in life—there are always exceptions to the rules, but the chances are you are not going to miss the love of your life, your soul mate, by following these landmarks of online dating. They will save you a lot of time and aggravation as they prevent you from meeting a lot of bad apples, so at least you won't get discouraged about online dating and the chances of meeting someone that way.

- *The "pretty boy":* If a guy's profile includes a gallery of photos in which he looks as if he's modeling—shirtless, flexed muscles, looking too cool for school—he's too cool for you. You should know what he's looking for. You can see these guys in the bars. They're just like women who dress sleazy to try to get anyone's attention. You know what kind of guy these women attract and what kind of guys will approach them—the guys who are looking for a hit and run with no relationship, not even staying overnight. Men like that are online to find some easy sex. Women who contact them will do so because of their looks. Now they may think they are just as hot as he is, which is fine, but it's looks that he's selling, and that's what you're buying and vice versa. He gets on the computer during the week, which is a lot less effort and hassle than the bar scene. He doesn't have to work hard, doesn't have to figure out which woman is looking for something serious and which one he can play with. On the computer he won't get stuck with the wrong women for most of the evening. He doesn't have to buy drinks; the experience costs him nothing. He's not even restricted to talking to only one woman at a time. He can be responding to other women while he's e-mailing you. So if you contact him or respond to his e-mail, it's perfect weekday encounters for him. He doesn't have to go through the empty bars on weekdays looking for someone. He won't be tired in the morning going to work, and he's not spending any money. How can he go wrong? Now when you go out with him, chances are you are not getting a Friday and Saturday night no matter how well it goes. You may get a weeknight and one weekend night, but not both weekend nights. The other nights he will be on another date or going out with his buddies to a club for some live action—the old fashioned way of hunting. He's shopping around, and he will be for a long time to come. Even after a few dates, you won't get both weekend nights. He'll still be looking around for something better, or more likely something different. He will not feel bad about sleeping with three women at the same time, and still he will try to keep a weekend free. None of the women he's with will make him feel that there's nothing better than you out there. You can even be the best thing he can get, but you can't be something different every night, and that's what he's looking for. Nothing personal—he's just fulfilling his needs: variety, fun, freedom, challenge, and the excitement of the hunt.

- *The older guy who's after younger women:* A man's profile must include the age of the women he is interested in meeting. If he's in his forties and looking for a woman who's twenty, "Houston we have a problem!" This man figures that there are some young women who like older guys, either for things they can do or provide for them, or any other reason. He knows they are out there. So while he's kind of looking for someone serious to come along, he doesn't want to miss an opportunity to get some tight young piece of ass. Think about it. What will a forty-five-year-old man have in common with a woman who is twenty-something? Forget about the Hollywood stories; they are usually short lived. Forget about "age doesn't matter." It usually does. She may like that he can provide for her, maybe take her places, even maybe provide good conversation. She may like a man with life knowledge and experience, but it doesn't matter what attracted her to him. Ask yourself what would attract him to her? Do you really think that he can have an intelligent conversation about life experiences, stories from the past, experience of a broken marriage, challenges of raising kids, the things we value in life now, the way we see our future, our path in life after we've been faced with life's surprises? Could they discuss the way they think now compared to the way they thought twenty years ago when they were still growing up and finding themselves, figuring out who they were. As much in common as a forty-year-old woman has with a twenty-year-old boy, so does a forty-year-old man have with a twenty-year-old girl. That man is not ready; he still values the thrill of the chase and the hunt. He still feels the accomplishment of getting something that young, something he shouldn't be able to attract. He still thrives on the feeling "I still got it," and he needs recognition from others, especially women, to value himself as a man. Be aware of that. Nothing is 100 percent; there are always exceptions to the rule, but even if he is partially open to that kind of relationship, even if it's the last option for him, most likely he doesn't have all his partying days behind him. He may not be as committed to finding that one person for life as you are. A man looking for a serious relationship is looking for a woman closer to his own age. The age of a woman he considers going out with is often an indication of his intentions. So, again, just be aware of this. If you go for a relationship with a man who doesn't care about a woman's age, know that you may be replaced by a new model, or if you're lucky maybe just cheated on with one.

Profiles of older men are usually more direct than profiles of younger guys. Men in their fifties will ask for certain things—expectations they have from a woman they want to meet. Men in their thirties and forties more often won't do this. How can a man say he's looking for a serious relationship—for a partner to share his life with—if he doesn't know what he wants from a woman? What kind of person is he looking for? What does he expect from her? A man should have some standards too. He should list what kind of women interests him. Men with standards have expectations from women because they know what they themselves bring into the relationship, and they want just as much back. They know what they like to do, and they want a woman who has similar interests so they can enjoy those things together. They don't want someone to be compromising all the time. The online dating sites give a man so many options and possibilities to list things they are looking for from a woman. He can write about what kind of woman will complement him. He has had to learn something throughout his life about himself and his likes and dislikes in a relationship. This helps him to know what he's looking for. Does it matter to him if a woman drinks, smokes, or does drugs? Is she career oriented or is she a stay-at-home mom? Does she like to stay home, put on comfortable clothes, lie down and watch a movie? Or would she rather dress up and go to a show or the theatre ... travel, and be out and about? Is he so desperate that any woman will do, and he will try to change accordingly? Are you that desperate that that kind of a man will do?

- *The guy who tries to impress you:* When they talk about their successful careers and their accomplishments—show pictures of their toys and Las Vegas trips—they are telling you they can take care of you and want to take you to fancy dinners. Right away that's a red flag. These are the same "muscle" guys from the first paragraph. They're just using different tools. Their looks are probably gone (or they never had them), but their money is there. If that's what you want, if you are impressed by that, chances are he can impress someone else later on. If that's what it is about with him, he can always "upgrade" to someone else. He's probably done it before, and he's probably trying to replace someone else with you right now. The grass is always greener on the other side for a man who is not set in his ways regarding what he wants, for a man who doesn't love you enough, for a man who focuses only on the looks and fun that you bring to the relationship. You will not feel special to a man like that. He will move to on to something "better" sooner or later.

So these will be your guidelines and the red flags to look out for when you read someone's profile or respond to an e-mail. Ask many questions if you're interested. It should be easier for a man to answer your questions online rather than in person, because he will have time to think about what he wants to say. Find out what he's really looking for before you give out too much info about yourself. Talk about life experiences—nothing too personal, but talk about trips, birthdays, celebrations, hobbies. Try to get stories out of him, some of the things that he has done ... some of his experiences. Men lie better when we are answering direct questions than if we are describing life experiences. It is very difficult to figure out if people are lying on their profiles or even from the few e-mails you may exchange in the beginning. That is why I believe that Internet dating is a blessing for men. You have to pay attention to certain things and see them as they are, not as you wish them to be. Don't ignore them, because you don't want to believe that they mean anything.

So remember: The age of the woman he wants to date can indicate his intentions. If he is trying to impress you with his looks and his toys, it may all be about him and his ego. Listen to his words and actions. Does he say he's adventurous and loves to try new things but then always goes to the same place for vacation? Does he say, "I work hard and play hard" but has nothing to show for it either in terms of money or stories of great experiences he's lived through? He may say family is very important to him, but life is so crazy and he is so busy that he only sees them on holidays. Always try to determine if his actions back up his words—or is he just saying what he thinks you want to hear? As we get older we do grow and change, but there is a lot to find out about him from his past and the way he talks about it now, as well as what he tells you he wants from the future.

Now let's go to your profile. Ladies, when you write your profile, you are not sharing feelings with your girlfriends. More information will not give us a better picture of your personality other than the fact that you love to talk. Don't use ten words to describe the same quality. You don't have to say genuine, loyal, honest, trustworthy … blah blah blah. Guys will just skip reading and go back to your picture. No matter what your life experiences are, describe them with fewer words, and leave a little mystery. You want to tickle his imagination. We will just forget about all the things you write if you write a long profile. We will simply focus on your picture. There is nothing left to make us intrigued. Trust me on that one.

Try something like this: *You say:* I'm an active fit woman and take great pride in it; I'm comfortable in my own skin, self-confident and not intimidated by anyone. I'm looking for a man to complete my life as I would his and not for a man to give my life meaning. *I Read:* She's in shape; she works out and always will. She likes being active and trying new things. She knows what she wants, and she doesn't need a man but would love one. She will make her man feel special but not essential and always interested in her. I would have to earn everything, but the reward would be great. Only a really confident man who knows how to treat a woman will be able to get her. She will not be taken for granted at any stage of the relationship; she's the ultimate prize.

You say: I skied at Whistler, scuba dove in the Bahamas, made love in the ocean. I have enjoyed shows like *Les Misérables*, but have also spent weekends in bed naked in the arms of a man I love. Looking to find that again. *I Read:* I'm not reading. I'm drooling and e-mailing you. You love to travel, you like all kinds of sports, trying new things, trying new adventures. One night you will get all dolled up for me to have on my arm for a night on the town, and another night we can stay home for a romantic, exciting, passionate evening. This woman will require a man in every sense of the word to seduce her, and the reward will be amazing. Every man wants to feel special; every man wants to feel that he has a woman no other man can have. Women are picky, and men will want to be the one she picks. Men will understand what is expected of them if she is to become interested. He needs to be in shape, enjoy an active life, be adventurous, be romantic and very attentive, be confident of himself, have his life in order, be ready to share with someone special—respectfully, equally, and romantically. Having a woman like that will make him an even better man.

If you don't believe me, make two profiles. Put a wig on, take similar pictures, and put your kind of profile under one picture and my kind of profile under the other. Let's see what sort of man your profile will attract. Let's see the quality of candidates either one will get. Now I know all of you didn't do all that traveling and have all those adventures, but you are not all looking for the same kind of man either. Don't sell yourself short. There are surely great experiences in your life, and they don't have to be exotic. If you're a homebody maybe you like to cook, maybe you have experienced some great cuisine somewhere, maybe you love going to the cottage. You love early mornings and tranquil moments by the water at sunrise. Maybe you saved a hurt animal. Share your experiences and the memorable moments of your life. The things you have done in your life are not in competition with someone else's. Theirs may be exotic, wild, and adventurous, but your experiences are the ones that made you happy. Your hobbies give you enjoyment, and you're looking for a man who enjoys the same things you do. So don't think there is nothing in your past to cherish and brag about. Embrace what makes you happy and put it out there. Share your experiences, what your interests are, and what you love to do in your free time. It will sound like a great profile to somebody. Share the things that you have done, and show what you enjoy doing in your free time.

Don't sell yourself short, but don't write a novel. Don't put everything out there either; leave some things for the man to find out when he meets you. There has to be a little bit of mystery.

CHAPTER 6

Dating More than One Man

This is a very unfamiliar concept for most women. They don't think it's right; they feel that, if they date more than one man at a time, that they're not true to themselves, who they are, and what they believe in. They think it's not fair to the men they are dating. Well what does it really mean to date someone? When do you cross that line of actually starting to date? You met someone for coffee. You talked for an hour and you are dating now? Did you ask him to be exclusive to you? Did you talk about it? How does it happen? I'll tell you one thing—it takes a little more than that for a man to consider himself in a relationship.

So what determines that you are "seeing someone"? Is half an hour for coffee and an agreement to meet again enough? Or does it begin once you share a physical relationship? It is a personal choice—whatever you are comfortable with. I'm just saying push it back a little bit if you can. Wait a little bit longer to consider yourself in a relationship. It will give you a better perspective on things. You only met that man briefly once or twice, and you're already putting all your dating eggs into one basket. You will wait to sleep with him until you feel he may be the last man you'll want to be with, but you are ready to discard all other opportunities after only a half an hour's worth of conversation over coffee? It doesn't make sense. Keep your options open until you feel he maybe the right one. Another indicator is that you are ready to make love with him.

Especially if you have been alone for a while, you need to explore. When you have been denied something for some time, there is more desire in you to have it. If you got stuck on a deserted island and you didn't have a sip of water for three days, the next glass of water would taste the best ever. So if you haven't dated for a period of time, the next date may easily seem much better than it really is. You don't want your good judgment to get overpowered by a pure desire. You don't want to fall in love with the concept of a relationship instead of with the man you are with. Your expectations of a man will become lower, you will not want to be demanding, and you will be ready to compromise. If you have to compromise from the beginning, your relationship will not be too promising.

Now, to find a great man, you have to put yourself in a position to meet him. You have to be approachable. You are looking for that special man for you, someone who will fulfill your needs, someone who has similar interests in life to yours, but someone who will also let you be yourself and embrace you as you are. So you need to keep your head straight. Remember what you are looking for, and don't start compromising from the beginning. Don't be a victim of pure desire for a relationship. It takes some women less time to commit to a man than it does for them to pick a wedding dress. Think about it, a woman will search catalogs, visit many wedding dress stores, and even go to different cities looking for the perfect dress. She will try on many dresses. She will have her girlfriends come to help pick the right one. She will have family members give them suggestions before they make the choice. And yet she's ready to commit to a guy after two dates? How does that make sense? He's someone she's picking for life, and the dress is for one day only.

Women often commit to a man too soon and with blinders on. Even when your girlfriends tell you he's not nice to you, he's not treating you well, you shouldn't trust him, you don't want to listen to them. How many times have you heard a woman say, "He really loves me. He's different when we're alone. You don't know him like I do"? That is falling in love with the relationship and not the man. Craving that connection with someone, needing a bond, can become overwhelming sometimes, and can dull a person's rationally. All I want to say is, avoid being in that state of mind when you're picking the person to be with. Use your head more than your heart in the beginning. If it's the right man, the heart will take over. And don't worry; you won't be able to stop it.

Men don't dream of their weddings from the time they are little boys. We don't dream of it two days before it happens, never mind twenty years before. If you ask a guy if he's single after he's had three dates with someone he'll say, "Yes." Most women will say, "I'm seeing someone." A man's attitude about those previous dates is, "Let's see what happens and we'll go from there." He leaves room for someone better to come along; he isn't committed. He'll see how it goes, and when he's really sure, then he'll commit. That usually takes more than a couple of dates.

Women are already working on the relationship after three dates. They are creating bonds. They think they have to be committed to know if he is the right man. Their minds are already closed to anyone else. They think, *How can I know if he's the right person if I'm not all in?* So I'm just telling you, think like men do: *Let's see what happens.* Two dates is not worth you're full effort. It's okay to put effort in something that you really want. You want a great pair of red shoes. You try on a pair of black shoes that you really love. They feel great and look great. They come in red, but someone just bought the last pair in your size. The sales clerk says they are in stock in a store fifty miles away. You will mostly likely get in your car and go get them. On the other hand, if you weren't certain the shoes fit properly, or you didn't know for certain that they were available in the other store, you probably wouldn't drive fifty miles in an effort to find out. It should be the same with the man you're dating—don't put too much effort until you're sure he's worth it.

A woman who is approachable, who goes out on more than one date and keeps her options open until she's sure, is like a woman looking ahead to many wedding dresses in many stores. She has the opportunity to find just the right one. A woman with one store to pick from will get in, find something, and hope that she can alter it to be the way she wants it to be. She hopes she will be able to make it fit, even if it's not perfect right now. She's convinced that she can work on it. Well don't be. Men don't need fixing; men aren't a project you can work on. They will not turn out "right." Someone will have to compromise, someone will be unhappy, and the chances are that it will be you.

So there's nothing wrong with dating more than one person at a time. Even if your first date with someone was really good, it doesn't matter. It's supposed to be good; it's a first date. All the dates should be great. They should flow. You should feel comfortable. It should be easy. Remember, you are not building a space ship; you're going out on a date. You are equipped with the instincts and rationale; don't let the lack of dating disable them. Don't let the desire for companionship blind you. Go on dates, have fun, let the man ask for your time, for your commitment. He approached you first. He chased you. He should be the ones asking first to be exclusive, not the other way around. You have all the power, so use it.

Quiz

1. How often are you approached by a man?

    a.   Once a month or less.
    b.   Two to five times a month.
    c.   All the time.

2. When approached you:

    b. Don't even recognize the approach as such.

    c. Engage in conversation.

    a. Make it as short as possible.

3. If you like the guy you will:

    b. Try to run into him again (same place, same time).

    a. Shrug it off and think he is probably married.

    c. Discretely let him know where he could run into you again.

4. Your dates mostly come through:

    a. Friends and family.

    b. Work and social events.

    c. All different occasions.

5. When and how you meet someone is:

    a. Very important to you.

    c. Not important at all.

    b. Might raise a red flag but is not a deal breaker.

You will notice that the letters are mixed around. The reason is that people expect the "right" answer in a quiz to always be in the same order, either first, middle or last, so we fall in a trap of answering in the order of what we anticipate to be the right answer. That is the reason I mixed up the letters: I want you to answer what you really think is the right answer for you.

If you answered mostly A, men may be having trouble approaching you. It may not be that your personality is difficult, but you need to let people meet you and see what you're all about. Try to meet new people even if you're shy. Do it through your friends and at events at which you feel comfortable.

If you answered mostly B, you're open to meeting new people, but not by your own initiative, and you probably don't give much thought about meeting someone new. You need to be pursued for a while to even consider that the relationship might be something more than just an acquaintance. There's nothing wrong with being careful, but then again there's nothing wrong with going on a date to find out if could be anything more.

If you answered mostly C, you're a social butterfly. Your problem is not meeting new people but what comes after that. You're a big a step ahead of many women by being approachable. You just have to figure out which one of those men is the right man for you.

CHAPTER 7

Setting Up a First Date

There are two big factors about setting up your first date. It may never occur to you that you can find out a lot of things and save yourself a lot of aggravation just by the way you set up your first date. Remember, the ball is in your corner, and you want to keep it that way. He approached you: He made the first contact. He wants you. You may want to meet him as well, but remember that your reasons may be different from his. You still don't know anything about him; the more charming he is, the harder it will be to figure him out. Always assume that he has played this game before. Even if you say that you are not into playing games and you're looking for a serious relationship, your words will mean nothing to him.

If he finds you attractive (and he does, that's why he approached you) he will not start feeling bad about his intentions just because you say you are looking for a serious relationship. He will not apologize and walk away if his intentions are not honorable. If he walked away every time he met a woman who wants more than just casual sex, he would be a very lonely man. If that's all he has planned for you—if all he wants is casual encounters—the fact that you say you aren't into that will not make him turn away. If he's married or just wants "friends with benefits," he won't admit it. You will have to figure that out for yourself. Once you do, you'll have to walk away. Always be ready to walk away.

His shortcomings are nothing you can work with or fix. Maybe you can fix his haircut or the way he dresses, but you can't fix his character flaws. Then again, they may not be flaws; he may just be at a different stage at his life than you are. He might not be looking for same things you are at this point in time. He's looking after his own needs and not yours—just as you are looking after yours and not his. You're looking for something else. You're not going to sleep with him just so he can fulfill his needs, so don't expect him to look after yours before his own. Be ready to walk away if it's not working for you. Dating is about quantity; quality will surface sooner or later.

Don't let your past dating experiences cripple your judgment. The number of dates you've had in the past has nothing to do with the date you're currently on. Ten bad dates doesn't mean you're difficult. One date in the last three months doesn't mean you should be thankful that someone finally asked you out.

When setting up your date, the first thing you want to do is pick a place. It should be a very public place, and preferably close to where he lives. If he tells you that he wants to go somewhere quiet so you can talk and get to know each other, he may not be as genuine as he sounds. Maybe there's a reason for it. Maybe there is a wife or longtime girlfriend in the picture, but he's still looking for some adventure or something fun to come along. Pick a nice public place—maybe a coffee shop or an eating area at a popular mall near where he lives. If you go to a restaurant, ask for a table by the window where people can see you as they walk by. Watch his reaction. Will he feel uncomfortable or will he not care? If you end up at the mall, tell him that you would like to visit a couple of shops so you can get something for your niece's birthday (any other excuse will do). Tell him you would like to continue the conversation with him while you do your errand. Now, if he has a problem with that—or the location you picked—maybe he doesn't want to be seen with you. He may be married. You two may be of different races or religions. Maybe his friends or family wouldn't approve if they saw you together. They might approach you and start asking questions. There could be many reasons that he doesn't want to be seen with you; the reason doesn't matter to you. All that matters is that you need to walk away and not even go on that date if he has a problem meeting you at the place you picked. He's not the man for you; it wasn't meant to be. Don't analyze it. Don't compromise. Just walk away from it. If you don't, you will pay for it later. Always remember, you have another date next week, or tomorrow, or whenever. Quantity will bring quality.

The next thing about your first date is the time of day or evening. He may calculate the risk of being caught at your chosen location and still go for it, so you need to give another little twist to your choice to make it a little more difficult for him to get away with something that you wouldn't want to deal with later on. It's the time of the date. Let's make sure it's not on a weeknight—not a night when he can tell someone (a wife) that he has to work late, and he's already dressed for a date. So it has to be a weekend. For a married man, the weekends are reserved for family, especially Saturday afternoons and evenings. Sunday brunch is also a good time. You can also let him know that you like to dress nicely when you go to the mall. Or, better yet, you can say that you have to go to an anniversary party or an opening night after you meet him. That will tell him that you will be dressed nicely, and he will be less likely to show up in running shoes and track pants. You don't want him to lie to someone and say that he's going golfing or helping a friend move if it's an afternoon date. Now there may be a chance that he has something to do that weekend and he can't see you, so the first thing you need to ask before setting up your date is if there is any time that is not good for him. Men don't usually make plans more than a week ahead, but he might have something that upcoming weekend. If he can't make it on the nearest weekend, schedule it for the following Saturday and tell him to call you to confirm on Thursday or Friday. Do not call him; let him call you. And when he does, apologize and tell him your girlfriend got you a surprise—maybe a day at the spa ... any excuse will do—and see if you can switch your date to Sunday. If he had to clear the Saturday with someone, it will be difficult for him to switch to Sunday on such short notice. By now he will find it too difficult to deceive you, and he will move on to easier prey.

Don't worry about it. Don't analyze the situation to decide if you made it too hard. If he had honest intentions and really wanted to get to know you, you would still be going on a date. Just think of it as avoiding disappointment later on.

When you talk to him on the phone, don't seem too eager to see him, but don't sound not interested at all. Let him know that you would really like to meet him and find out more about him and see where it goes. Men like to feel wanted just as women do, but the important thing is not to make him the center of your world right now, but still let him feel that he could be one day. So the time and place are your two best strategies for separating the bad apples. That will help you to get rid of the guys whose intentions are not like yours. Profile headlines like "No head games, no players, looking for a real genuine man" will not help you out. In the perfect world, maybe, but then again in a perfect world you would already have what you wished for. Headlines like that may just put a challenge in front of an alpha male who is looking for some excitement. When you say, "I'm a good judge of character. I'll figure you out," it's just like a cherry on top. Trust me on this, if you haven't lived a life of deception and manipulation, you will not know what the hell happened when you are a victim of that sort of behavior. You will wonder how you could have been so wrong about someone when you were so sure about your ability to recognize a man's intentions. Pretty soon you'll be calling every man a dog because of the actions of one who tricked you. No matter what we do in life, there is always someone out there better at it than we are, so just take one step at a time. Remember, you have all the power. You control the situation, and you have to figure him out. Do what you can to weed out the players. Follow your instincts and the strategies I give you in this book. Let your brain lead you, and let your heart follow, until it's time for the roles to reverse. You may want to meet him once briefly for coffee to see if there is any chemistry, to see if he is worth the effort, but once you do, you need to determine how interested and available he is.

Chapter 8

First Date

Once you pick the location and the time of your first date and he seems fine with it, all you will have is some piece of mind that he is decent company. That doesn't mean that you're getting married in three months; it just means that you're both interested and want to see if anything real will come out of your meeting. You're both available and looking for that significant other, and you may both be great people, but still not great for each other. Many men will fall into the trap of trying to impress a woman. They will be on their best behavior, but that kind of attention cannot be sustained forever, and once he thinks he has your heart, the effort on his part may wither away. It's human nature to take others for granted if we are allowed to. You can't pretend to be something you are not for the rest of your life.

You need to try to bring conversation down to daily life—small talk about interests and life experiences. Don't talk at all about money and very little about work. If you're not a gold digger, you don't care how much money he makes or what he has, and if he's looking for a long-term relationship, he's looking for a genuine woman who won't care about that. If he's talking about money too much, he's trying to impress you, to buy your affection. Remember, anything (including a woman) that can be bought can be replaced later by a better product.

Sometimes a man is uncomfortable meeting a woman for the first time so he wants to talk about something he is familiar with or maybe something that has worked for him before. Obviously it didn't work too well, because he is here on another first date, so give him a break. You can nicely help him understand that you want to know who he is not what he does for a living. His job should not define who he is; there should be more about him than his work. If he keeps going back to his success story and the toys he has, you know what you are dealing with. There is nothing more to him but his job, his money, his career, and you'll never be the number one in his life.

Now let's compare a first date to a job interview. When you are young and you are going for your first job interview, you don't ask too many questions. You are trying to sell yourself ... to present yourself in the way you think your employer would like to see you. He has all the power in his hands. He's the one giving you a chance. You don't ask too much about benefits, sick days, vacation, or company policies. The main thing for you is to get the job, to get the opportunity to prove yourself, to learn and get some experience so you can advance, make more money, and make a future for yourself. Once you're established in your field, when you are really good at what you do, you're in demand and you can choose where you want to work. Things have changed by then, and the interview becomes more like a merger, a coming together for the benefit of both parties. Now you want to know what this company has to offer you because you know what you are bringing in. You want to see your work place, how the employees are being treated, what the company policies are, and so forth. You want to see what your future could be with the company. I know this doesn't sound too romantic, but remember, it's only your first date and you should treat it as that. You're not desperate. You're not looking for a handout. You know what your standards are and how you want to be treated. You will pay attention to how your date is treating you. Does he let you walk in front of him? Does he open doors for you ... let you sit down first?

All these little things show respect for you as a woman and a lady. Now, also, how he treats others is very important—the waitresses in the restaurant, the sales people in stores, and people around him in general. You two complement each other, and the things he does and the way he behaves will reflect on you. If he's rude and arrogant to people around him, they will be thinking, *What is she doing with a jerk like that?* The first answer that comes to their minds most likely will be that he's got the money, and what does that make you? Do you want to be seen that way? Is he going to treat your friends like that? How about your family members? There are many things to consider.

Now let's assume that everything is going well. It's good to have a few subjects to talk about ready before you meet. There should be a few things you want to ask him, but remember it's conversation, not an interrogation.

- Try not to ask questions that can be answered with a simple yes or no, and try not to answer that way yourself.
- Before you go out, write down some things that you are interested in talking about. The better prepared you are, the more you will find out about him. He will probably be a little bit careful not to take a hard stance before he knows where you stand on certain issues. Some issues may not even be important to him. He may never really have thought about them, but you might stand strongly on one side of the issue, so he will not want to upset you over something that he doesn't really care about.
- Don't go into heavy topics like gay marriage, immigration policies, and things of that nature. It's not that they aren't important, but they aren't good conversation points for a first date. Such topics make you look cold and calculated. He will feel as if he's being interrogated, and that is not what he came out for.

- Here are some safe and interesting topics of conversation for a first date:
- What is the most memorable experience in your life?
- What was your best vacation ever?
- What is your background? (If he came to your country as an adult, perhaps he experienced the shock of a different culture. Perhaps he might talk about things that are different now from the way they are in his homeland, good or bad.)
- What was your first love like? (Never ask about his latest one. You don't care, and you don't want to be compared to her.)
- Is there anything you would change if you could go back five, ten, or twenty years?
- What would you do if you won $5 million? What about $100 million? (You would see how much of a difference his life would be with more money. Would he help more people or still just the family?)

These things are harder to lie about than direct questions like, "Are you looking for one person for life or are you still playing the field?" When you're listening to his answers, you should be able to get some feeling as to what he's about. For example if he says he'd give all of his lottery winnings to humanitarian purposes, that's just as bad as saying he wouldn't help anyone—because he's probably lying. So, have few things ready to talk about. If he's genuine, your questions will make him more comfortable, and the conversation should flow. Let him talk. You learn nothing when you talk, only when you listen. Remember you have the power, you know where you're going, and you know what you want.

Here's a little analogy: Be a bus, not a taxi. A bus takes a specific route. People get on and get off, but they always travel the same prescribed route the bus takes. Nobody tells the bus driver to alter the route by taking a different street. If the bus isn't going by your destination, take a different bus. On the other hand, taxis pick up people wherever they are and take them wherever they want to go. A taxi driver will take a different street if you tell him to, and make stops where you tell him to. After he drops you off, he doesn't know his next route; he just waits for someone to hop in and tell him where to go. Now, you know where you're going in your life. You don't need a man to tell you which way to go or where to stop. You don't need a man to tell you where you need to go. Believe in that and assert yourself that way from the beginning. Be a bus.

And another thing, there should be no cell phones on your date. You should be the focus of his attention and the only person in the room for him. Only you can establish that. If he answers his phone while you're on your date, just give him a look. When he is finished (very quickly, hopefully) just say, "I hope that won't happen again" or "Maybe we should cut this date short." You have better things to do than listen to his phone conversations. My neighbor, Rick, told me my favorite cell phone first date story. He took Tina to a restaurant. Halfway through the meal, he answered his phone and didn't try to cut the conversation short. A couple minutes into the call, Tina went to the washroom. On her way back to the table, she stopped by the bar where a lot of guys were watching a game. She made a little comment to them, and the guys jumped at the chance to have a conversation with her. She made Rick wait fifteen minutes before she went back to the table. After that, he set his phone to vibrate mode, and he let all calls go to voicemail. You need a little bit of guts for that one, but you have to remember that, if he's doing that on a first date, it will only get worse later on. So don't be afraid to let the date go bad. Don't be afraid to walk away. You will either save yourself from a lot of aggravation later on, or he will learn real fast. You have the power, so don't give it up.

Now, when it comes to the dinner, he must to pay. There's no going Dutch; it's his responsibility to pay. If the date is going well and you decide to go for coffee afterward, you should offer to pay, but offer sincerely; don't just throw it out there. He may not let you pay anyway, but he will appreciate the thought—it's only a few bucks. You had a great evening, and you are showing your appreciation. It will also show that you don't need his money; you look to pay your own way but you let him be a gentleman.

Letting him be a gentleman and appreciating his intentions also shows that you will carry yourself as a lady. Now, as I suggested, if you're having lunch or dinner in a mall, ask him if he would mind going with you to buy something. If he agrees to go (and most likely he will), it's because he's interested. He still doesn't feel as if he "has" you, and he's still not sure that there will be another date. He still wants to assert himself in your mind so that he will have a better chance of a second date. You should go to the store that reflects your interests and the topics you talked about. If he said he's interested in cooking, he should be able to interact with you when you're picking out a gift at a culinary store. If you talked about kids, you will see if he gets involved with helping you find something for your niece or nephew—or will all that be left to you once you two have kids? Does he hate going to the store but will still do it for you? Or just go nuts—take him to Victoria's Secret and see if he will be uncomfortable or playful. You can learn a lot about people when you take them out of their comfort zones. If he decides to wait outside, let him wait a little longer. He could have helped you to make a choice, and the errand would have taken less time, so it's okay to make him to wait a little longer. When you like someone you will do things with him or her even if you don't really like doing them, just to be with that person. Down the road in life, there will be a lot of chores, and if you have to do them all on your own you won't be too happy. It's good to see if he's ready to help. Will he ever make himself available so you two can get some free time together—or even some free time for you? Will all these things be left for you to do?

When the date is over, thank him. Let him know you had a really good time—if you did, of course. You didn't have an amazing time or an incredible time, just a really good time. Let him say, "Let's do it again." Let him ask you out. You have given him enough information to know that you would like to go out with him again.

Don't embarrass yourself by asking him; maybe he doesn't want to go out with you!

When he asks you to go out again just tell him to give you a call so you can set up another date. Don't give him a day that you're free, and definitely don't tell him that you're free anytime. There is no need to set up a second date the same night. Let him call you. Let him put forth the effort. Remember, don't give away the power. He still needs to chase you, but let him know that you usually make your plans ahead of time. You will see if he's going to play the "three-day-wait card" before he calls. And if he does, oh well, guess what? Your girlfriend called yesterday, and you've made plans already. Don't be angry. Don't be rude. And don't explain where you're going. All he needs to know is that he's late; all he needs to know is that you're not waiting for him. Two can play that game. Be polite. Be nice. He doesn't need to know that you are making a point. No, you have a life to live. You don't have time to wait around for anyone.

If he waits three days to call you, do not give him the upcoming weekend. Just think like this: maybe he was waiting to see what options he had for weekend plans, and you were plan B. If you knew for a fact that you were not his first choice, would you be ready to jump as soon as he called? You don't know why he didn't call earlier, and you don't care. Stop thinking and analyzing. Maybe he didn't want to scare you away, or maybe he thought that was the appropriate time to call, or maybe he was too busy. Stop giving him the benefit of the doubt. The real truth is that he followed the three-day rule. That rule was not made by naïve humble nice guys; it was made by real alpha males. It's one of many steps that men use to control and set up future dynamics and the balance of power in their relationships. If you read a book called *How To Manipulate a Woman To Do Everything for You Like a Servant*, and one of the rules was wait three days after a date before you call, what would you think then? Would you still be so eager to make excuses for him? Tell him to call you on Sunday, and you can talk then. When he calls make sure you don't pick up. Let him leave a message. If he does, call him the following evening, apologize that you hadn't been able to call him earlier. Don't give any reasons, and if he comments on it, say, "Maybe I should have waited three days to call back." Just say, "Sorry I didn't have my phone with me." That's all the explanation he deserves at that point. If he doesn't leave a message, don't call him back. If he calls again, answer the phone. If he says he called before, say you didn't know, because he didn't leave a message. Don't worry. He will get *your* message loud and clear.

CHAPTER 9

Second Date

Now the second date depends on how the first date went. It depends on when he called you again, and all the things that happened from the moment you first met until now. If you're still interested, you will proceed with this date. You've already had a chance to show him what you're all about, and he may not be trying to pull the wool over your eyes. He could be really interested in you. Either he sees you as someone he could seriously proceed with, or he's still not convinced that he cannot play you.

So here a few thoughts. If he's trying to play you, you can show him that everything he can do, you can do better. Let him pick the location for a second date. Be open minded and dress nicely. I mean, very nicely ... sexy. And that is sexy appropriate to your age. Don't try to look twenty if you're forty. A woman's attraction is more than the eye can see. Tighter skirts or jeans can be sexy without revealing too much. High heels are always sexy. If you present your expectations with regard to how you want to be treated ... if you set your standards right, he will not take your sexy attire as a signal that you are ready to put out that night. He will think that it will be worth waiting for. I don't recommend that you allow him to pick you up. If you're still not sure about him, you should be able to leave at any time if things don't go well. Let's go through a few tricks he might try if you were to allow him to pick you up. One of them is arriving early, especially in the wintertime. He may say he wanted to make sure he wasn't late, so he ended up coming half an hour early. Of course you're not ready, and you feel bad leaving him in the car to wait, especially in the cold. In instances like this, the second date becomes the last date when a woman lets him into her home, because if she really likes him, they might end up sleeping together. If that was all he wanted, he will be gone for good, which is fine, but you might not feel too good about yourself. If he was a good guy, the experience will make him reevaluate everything you said on the first date. Actions speak louder than words. You will make love to him when you decide to and on your terms and not because he charmed you into it. So if he shows up early, just tell him where the closest coffee shop is. Say you will call him when you're ready, which will now be twenty minutes later than you originally agreed. He will understand whom he's trying to play, and if he leaves, well he came to see you just to get lucky anyway, so don't worry about it. If he calls you later and expresses the fact that he is upset about how long you made him wait, ask him straight out if he really was thinking that he might get into your home and get lucky. Tell him you date men, not boys who still need their egos satisfied and who measure their manhood by the number of women they have slept with. It doesn't matter if you're first date was great; it just means it took two dates for his true colors to come out. He will be charming only until he gets what he wants.

Now if by some miracle you're still interested and he's really trying to make it up to you, tell him that you will text him and let him know where you will be the following Friday with your girlfriends. He can meet you there. Then text him that Friday evening just before you go out. This way he will have to drop all his plans, because he wouldn't even have been sure that you would actually call him. Now if he was really sorry for what happened and if there was the slightest chance that the bad part of your last encounter was a misunderstanding, he will meet up with you. He will know he has to meet you in the company of your friends. He will assume you have told them what a jerk he was. He will expect dirty looks. If he knows he was wrong and really wants to make it up to you, he will take it. Make him work for a while, but then let it go. He won't try to pull anything like that again. He will be very aware of his actions and make sure not to send out any mixed signals. He should have a clear picture by now of who you are and what kind of a man you're looking for. He will also know that you are worth all the effort that's needed to be walking with you side by side.

Now if he really has to use your washroom, and you have decided to let him into your home (which you shouldn't), make sure that when he comes out you're standing by the door in your coat and shoes ready to go. Don't wait for him on the couch. You two are going out for a date. Key words are *going out*. Even though you think you know how to handle him, it's still a test. If he just wanted sex, he will be disappointed that he couldn't close and that he could not get lucky even though he was in your house already. He will think you make it too difficult for him to get what he wants. He will probably cut the date short and never call again, but at least you'll know what he's looking for. If that's not his intention and your date with him continues, you're really presenting a challenge now. He sees you standing by the door, and he knows that you are aware of the possible scenarios that could develop now that he is in your house. He sees you in control of a situation, and that with you things don't "just happen." Things will only happen as you allow them to. You're not a pushover, and you don't allow yourself to be charmed or manipulated into doing something you don't want. Now you are a worthy opponent. Every alpha male is looking for an alpha female. So be that alpha female. Keep the control as long as you're not sure of his intentions. That's the only kind of women that can keep his attention … that can keep him interested.

Something that must be earned the hard way is always more appreciated than something gained through an easy accomplishment.

So be aware if you are not sure of his intentions yet. Look for the signs.

Let's say you had a very positive first date. Everything was great. He called you in good time afterward, and you're ready to go on a second date. He picks the location, and off you go. You can give him a little hug when you meet him, and maybe one of those "happy birthday" kisses on the cheek.

If he takes you somewhere stupid like a bowling alley or a sports bar to meet his buddies or anywhere you don't enjoy going, let him know. Give him a half an hour and say it's time to go. He should know where to take you if the first date was great. He should know what you enjoy doing. Tell him he can do the activities you don't enjoy with his buddies. Or he should find a tomboy, and that's not you. If he was listening on your first date, if he was paying attention to the conversation you were having, it should be easy for him to choose a venue for the second date where you will feel comfortable and find enjoyment. It's too early to interact with his buddies. You don't even know him yet, you shouldn't have to meet his friends. It's different if you come with your friends and he's with his, but that shouldn't happen on the second date. That happens later on when you know each other better, when it feels that you two are going to be dating for a while. There should be no buddies on either side on a second date. Let me put it this way, are you the focus of his attention with all his buddies around playing pool or bowling? Are you the most important person in the room to him? Are you being treated the way you want to be? If he includes his buddies on your date, he's testing you. He wants to see how you get along with them, because he plans that the two of you will spend quite a few evenings with his buddies. He wants to see if you will be good about it. He plans to hang out with them after you're his girlfriend. He's not letting go of his life as it is. You will just fill in a part of his life that he's missing, but you will not be the most important part of it. Now it depends on what you want and expect of your man and the relationship. You make a decision to stay or leave. Are you happy with where he brought you? Did you imagine your second date to be like this? Don't think, *It's only one date. Who cares?* If he doesn't care right now, do you think it will get better once he feels he has you, and you love him too much to leave? If you don't like where you are, it's time to go—with or without him.

If he takes you somewhere nice—a nice restaurant or maybe some place you mentioned on your first date—show your appreciation. Notice that he put thought into the date, that he remembered what you said you liked. Acknowledge the fact by touching him on the hand, saying thank you, and giving him a nice smile. You can let him know that you don't need a fancy restaurant (if that's where he chose) but that you do appreciate it. When it's the right company, any place will do. Don't dwell on it; acknowledge it a couple of times and let it go. You don't want him to think that nobody ever took you to a nice place. You don't want to leave an impression that you're impressed. Flattered, yes, but not impressed. What he is and who he is will be something that will impress you, not what he can do for you.

On the second date you should start to connect. He will be more relaxed around you, and he will open up more. It's still good to think of some topics ahead of time to talk about. You can talk about work a little bit, but the best topics are the ones that define you and him as individuals. The things we *like* to do will tell much more about us then the things that we *have* to do (like work). You will always find out more about people by talking about their hobbies and recreational interests rather than their job descriptions. You can talk about kids, siblings, the things that take up your free time and his, the things that show character by the way we treat the others in our lives. There's no need to talk about exes; there will be time for that, and one-sided stories don't have much meaning anyway. Breakups are never pleasant conversation, and the whole truth is never exposed in a situation like this. There's no purpose to or benefit from a conversation like that this early on. You want to find common interests. If you're adventurous, ask him about his wild side. Maybe he went bungee jumping or sky diving or white-water rafting. You can tell him about your adventures. If you're the artsy type, ask if likes to see plays or classical music performances, or take trips to historic sites. Maybe you're a cottage girl who enjoys nature, hiking, and picnics. As I mentioned before, ask him to use his imagination and tell you what he'd do if he found himself suddenly financially free. You will learn a lot about him.

The idea is to find as many common interests as you can. You don't want to depend on the "opposites attract" theory. It gets old too fast, and then someone has to compromise. If you want to compromise, compromise on your take-out order—pizza or Chinese. Are you going to rent a romantic movie or an action flick? Those are the compromises that we all make, and they don't affect our lives if we take turns making the choice. But if you pick big city lights and theatre nine times out of ten, and he chooses fishing and hunting in the same proportion, you will both be spending a lot of time on your own. If you want three kids and he doesn't want any, there will be a problem.

A relationship is not—and should not be—hard work if you two are compatible. What can be so hard if you both enjoy doing the same things? Sure there will be some bumps in the road. We all get mean sometimes because of the stresses of life, but it's not permanent. When you love someone, you don't want to see him or her hurt; you especially don't want to be the one causing the hurt. If you have a loving and respectful relationship, you can't be selfish—you *won't* be selfish, because you're partner will not tolerate it. You can get off track sometimes, but you'll get back on it fast, because the alternative is much worse. Losing your lover because you mistreated him or her is ten times worse than anything that's happening right now. Don't believe that relationships have to be hard work. Don't you expect to be better off with someone in your life than on your own? If you do not, then why get involved? You just want to work hard on it? You don't have enough things in your life you have to work hard on so you need to add a difficult relationship? If you start questioning whether you would be better off alone, you probably would.

If you want to spend 80 percent of your free time with that other person doing the things you both like, you don't want to spend that time compromising. The other 20 percent you can keep for your girlfriends, for shopping, or movie nights, or a book club. Whatever it is, it's just some time on your own—just as he has his buddies and his hobbies or sports. All the other times you should be enjoying doing things together and not working hard on your relationship, unless you two are just getting together to save on necessities of life like rent, gas, and electric bills. You want to have similar interests so you can spend time—happily—together. That is why it is very important to look for that similarity from the very beginning. What are you going to do together in five, ten, or twenty years when all this "getting to know each other" has gone by the boards? How are you going to spend your free time—will you be together, or will you have separate activities and hobbies?

That's why it's very important for you to fall in love with a man who suits you rather than to fall in love with the concept of being in a relationship. Just not wanting to be alone is not the best reason to begin a relationship, so don't be motivated by that idea. You have to make sure that you want to be with *him* and not with just *someone*. So after dinner, go somewhere for coffee or a walk ... just something to change the scenery. If you didn't pay for anything on the first date, pay now. Coffee or ice cream, it's not important. What's important is that you want to contribute in every aspect of the relationship. While good men don't expect a woman to do that, they do appreciate it when she chips in. Just as you wonder, in the beginning, if he just wants to sleep with you, he will wonder if you just want what he can provide for you. We always end up paying more. We will not tell you how much it costs, but we do want to know that you appreciate it and that you're not taking it for granted. It's nice when sometimes you surprise us and treat us. It shows that you care.

So let's assume that you feel great about how this is going. The two of you are connecting. Go ahead and show some affection. Give him a nice, real kiss when he makes his move, and he will if you look available and ready for it. Put your arms around him, pull him real close to you so you can feel if he's really happy to see you. It's okay. He won't think less of you. He will think the opposite, in fact. He will be thinking, *When is the next date going to be?* And it won't be to sleep with you. He's ready to wait, but he does want to make out with you in order to connect with you more, and to feel reassured that you are seriously choosing him. The threat that you might meet someone else between your dates is now smaller, and he feels surer about the two of you. It doesn't mean that he's got you now and that he can take your loyalty for granted. It only means that he can have you if he treats you right. If he doesn't, you can still slip away.

He can tell where he stands with you only through the way you act, so there's nothing wrong with a little hot encounter. It's well recommended. Just telling him that you like him won't work as well. Men tend to believe that a kiss is very personal to a woman. She won't kiss just anyone, and we start feeling a little special when we receive one. As I said, don't worry, he won't be thinking, *I've got her now.* As I said, he knows that you can still slip away, but you have just opened up a little more to him. This could be a great thing for him. This could mean he has found a woman he wants to marry, or the relationship could be over in seconds if he doesn't reach your standards and your expectations of him. You still have all the power, and he knows it. He still needs to seduce you; the hunt is not even close to being over. You're just enjoying his company so far, and you still don't need him. You have just made him feel a little bit special, but far from essential.

You should never be in a position in which you make him an essential part of your life. He's there to make your life better, not to save you. You don't need to be saved. Your attitude at this point should be, "Welcome aboard my bus. This is the route that it takes. If you're going the whole way, great. If you're not, there are a lot of stops, and you can get off on any one of them. Don't let the door hit you on your way off!"

Someone once said: "Love is giving someone the power to destroy you but trusting them not to." It takes time to trust someone that much. Don't do it after a few dates.

Quiz

1. When you meet someone new, you give him your number:

    a. Within half an hour if you like him. (10 points)
    b. By the end of the night. (5 points)
    c. Never (you always take his). (15 points)

2. If you take his number you will call:

    a. Never. (10 points)
    b. Sometimes. (5 points)
    c. Always. (15 points)

3. When you go on a first date:

    a. You decide where you go. (15 points)
    b. He decides. (5 points)
    c. Sometimes you decide, sometimes he does. (10 points)

4. On a first date you will dress:

    a. Appropriately for the location but still sexy. (15 points)
    b. Appropriately for the location but conservatively and comfortably. (5 points)
    c. To impress. (10 points)

5. On your date you always:

    a. Have a few things ready to talk about. (15 points)
    b. Just go with the flow. (10 points)
    c. Talk more than he does. (5 points)

6. How do you react to over complimenting?

    a. It always feels good. (10 points)
    b. It doesn't matter, it's part of the game. (5 points)
    c. It feels fake with only one purpose. (15 points)

7. At the end of the date you will kiss:

    a. Never. (10 points)
    b. Depends on the quality of the date. (15 points)
    c. Almost always to show him what he might have if he's the right man. (5 points)

40 to 65 points: You have some requirements and expectations from the man you date, but you are not consistent at it. The longer the relationship goes, the more you will be ready to compromise. You can't be bluffing your demands. Believe in them and don't be persuaded to change them or dismiss them. They have to be the most important thing to you.

70 to 95 points: You need to work on asserting yourself as a woman who knows what she wants and who is not easily manipulated by a man. Do not try to please a man so quickly, and don't be too anguished over trying to keep him. He is still far away from earning your full attention.

100 to 120 points: You don't give up control and power to a man. You know what you want and what your expectations of him are. Make sure that you recognize the good deeds he does, and don't forget to be worthy of his effort, not just difficult.

Chapter 10

Sex the First Time

Now this is one situation that cannot be influenced by timing. This is a personal decision that depends on the relationship that is developing between you two. Is there chemistry? How are things going? What kind of man are you dating? And most importantly, how do you feel about him? How can anyone say you should wait one or two or three months? In those three months you might have met five times altogether, or fifteen times. You are totally at a different stage of the relationship depending on how much time you have spent together rather than how long you have been dating. Even advising someone to wait for ten dates means nothing. What has been the quality of the dates? How are you connecting? You can feel closer to one person after three dates than you can after ten with someone else. The important thing is that you are engaging in sex not because of any rules or because you think you have to in order to keep him around. Nobody can tell you when the right time is but you.

Fifty years ago, it was considered improper to have sex before marriage; indeed, some people still live by that rule. But most people right now wouldn't agree with that. My advice is, don't follow any rules that would look just as stupid in twenty or thirty years' time as "no sex before marriage" sounds right now. How much time you will take depends only on how you feel about your partner, and sex will have no negative impact on your relationship if you handle the subject properly afterward. How much time goes by before you have intercourse is not as important as how it will affect your behavior, and that is where women make a mistake. That is a challenge you need to learn how to manage. Just look at sex as you look at any other life challenge. You can try to delay it and avoid it, but sooner or later life will throw you a curve ball and challenge you.

The important thing is to know how to handle the challenges, how to avoid being knocked down, and how to be ready for it. It's always better to prepare yourself for the upcoming challenges than to try to avoid them. Even after sleeping with someone for the first time, you still have the power if you know how to use it. Let me give you a personal story. My good friend Steve met Sasha in a bar—a typical meat market for adults. After a simple "Hi. How are you?" the conversation started flowing. They talked about the weirdest things—monogamy, feminism, chauvinism, and the things that other people meeting for the first time would not dare to discuss. They were both in their forties, had teenage children, and had recently divorced. They both felt that it was their time to enjoy life. She was sick and tired of house parties where men sit on one side smoking cigars, drinking, and discussing sports while the women sit together, gossiping, exchanging recipes, or discussing how much laundry they can fit into their new machines. Steve was the same; he couldn't see himself at home repaving the driveway, making wine, talking about his good old high school days, and playing an occasional weekend game of golf. They both wanted more out of life than the stale marriages they had been in. After all, life is not a rehearsal. You only get one chance, so you'd better make some memories. Steve used to say, "I won't die with a hundred million dollars in my bank account, but I will have a hundred good stories to tell."

So Steve and Sasha hit it off. They met again a few days later for dinner and ended up sleeping together. She didn't pretend it was her first time. She was passionate. She was good at it, and they had a great time. After a couple of hours she said, "I have to go." She gave him a kiss and went on her merry way. There was no, "I've never done this before. I hope you don't think less of me now. How was it for you? I had a great time." Nope. Nothing like that. No cuddling, no spooning, no staying for the night. She never asked Steve to call her. She never even asked if she'd see him again. I remember Steve telling me, "I was lying in bed thinking, *What just happened? Have I been used?*" She definitely left him wanting more. He knew right away he was in trouble. He wanted to see her again, even more now than before they'd had sex. She was even more of a mystery to him. He didn't think he "had" her now after sleeping with her. He was wondering if he was ever going to see her again. He started questioning himself. Had he been good in bed? Had she enjoyed herself? And if she had, how come she didn't ask for a next date?

She was an alpha female. She had got to him, and he knew it. They would meet once a week and have a great time. She was amazing—very passionate, and she made him feel like the best man in the world. But three to four hours later, she would leave. She made him feel incredibly special when they were together, but by the way she left each time, she made sure he didn't get the idea that he was essential. They would talk on the phone. She would call him, but only if he called her first. She never called first. It could be a week, and Steve always called first after a date. She used to say to him, "You're the hunter. If you're not hunting me, you will hunt someone else."

Four months into this relationship, they spent the entire night together for the first time. Do I need to tell you whose idea it was? See, Sasha never gave up her power. She was always very nice. She would tell him how much she enjoyed him. She would compliment him but never dwell on the praise. She made him feel really special, but she made it clear that once they went their separate ways, she had her life to live. She didn't wait for him to organize her free time. She didn't arrange her schedule around him; she fit him into her schedule.

It wouldn't matter if they slept together on their second, twentieth, or fiftieth date. It was her actions and her attitude afterward that counted, and that made Steve want her even more.

This woman is so hard to get, she doesn't need a man. It takes a special man to get a prize like that, and all men want to feel that they are the special ones, and they all want to have a prize that no other man can have. It's the ego in the hunter. It's a drive for an accomplishment, and if anyone could do it, and if any man could impress her, then what kind of an accomplishment would that really be?

Most men think that after sex they own the woman, and in most scenarios they do. But, ladies, that's your own fault. We just follow the signs that you're giving us. Women show men that they are the one that they want to be with now and forever and nobody else. It's as if he "ruined" her for all the other men, and she could never find anything like him again. That sort of thinking turns a woman into a convenience, into a booty call. You're not a challenge anymore, and you're the one who did it to yourself. You seem so desperate to have someone to be with that you'll do anything to keep him.

Okay, so the sex was great. You enjoyed it, but it doesn't mean you can't have the same thing with someone else. He should know without you telling him that there are plenty of volunteers out there to take his place. And that "thing" that he's so proud of? Well, God gave one of those to every man. It's called a penis. So instead of him thinking, *I got her*, he should be thinking, *I have to keep her. A woman like this doesn't come around too often and won't be single for a long time.*

So the power of your cookie is not really in holding it back, but in showing its real value. What is the value of anything if you don't use it? Don't make the mistake of holding back … the mistake of thinking you will scare him away with your skills. He might be thinking, *where did you learn all that?* but he will still love it. You don't have to pull out whips and chains the first time, but don't be shy either. If he makes any comment, just ask him if he's worried that he can't handle you. Tell him you know what you like, and if he's intimidated by it, maybe he should be looking for younger girls with no experience. They are the ones who will think he's the best ever no matter what. You don't date boys; you date men who know what they want and who are not intimidated by a woman or another man. I bet you he'll never bring that subject up again, and if something like that scares him away, so be it. You just got rid of someone who is insecure, who will be possessive of you, and who will always be asking you where you've been and getting upset with you if other men look at you, as if it's your fault.

Remember, the man you are with is supposed to make your life better. He's not supposed to try to change it. And he's not supposed to try to control you because of his own lack of confidence. He should let you be who you are. You're a bus going in a certain direction. You're not stranded in the middle of nowhere desperately waiting for a tow truck to save you. He doesn't give purpose or meaning to your life. You have that already. You're not in the middle of the ocean, and he's not a lifeboat. He's more like a cruise ship. Hopefully you will enjoy the cruise, but if you don't, the ship will stop at many ports, and you can just get off.

Quality comes from quantity. You don't have to sleep with everyone you go on a date with, but you do have to date. So, date and follow the guidelines. Learn to read the signs. Even if they don't make sense to you, remember that a man's behavior in general may not make sense to you just as your behavior doesn't make sense to us. So, ladies, do go on the date. It will help you stay in touch, and you can always learn something for the future. There's also another bright side to dating—with so many dinner dates, you're going to save a lot of money on groceries. There's an extra pair of shoes for you every month.

So I'll repeat again, the power of the cookie is how you handle yourself. Don't be afraid to walk away afterward. Don't start working too hard at a relationship; it will just become more work later. Love the man you're with and not the concept of a relationship. It's better to be alone than with the wrong person. When you're alone, there's a much better chance of meeting someone. Don't feel responsible if the relationship doesn't work out. Move on like men do, and believe something better will come along. It is generally perceived that a man will do anything to get into a woman's pants, and a woman will do anything to get a man to the altar. Change the perception.

Quiz

1. The first time you're intimate with someone, you:

    a. Are conservative.
    b. Let him know what you like.
    c. Take control.

2. During intercourse you are most concerned about:

    a. Pleasing him.
    b. Pleasing yourself.
    c. Pleasing both of you.

3. Immediately after intercourse you will:

    a. Start explaining yourself so as not to appear "easy."
    b. Compliment him no matter what.
    c. Be honest or not say anything.

4. Afterward:

    a. You're looking for round two.
    b. You're looking to please him.
    c. You want to lie around and cuddle.

5. When the date is coming to an end:

   a.   You initiate leaving.
   b.   He initiates leaving

6. The next contact is made:

   a.   By you calling.
   b.   By you texting.
   c.   By him.

7. Who asks for the next meeting?

   a.   You.
   b.   You always let him ask.

8. When he asks you:

   a.   Give him one available date within the week.
   b.   Say you're available any day.

9. Next meeting, if he's late, you:

   a.   Wait for him and tell him never to do it again.
   b.   Wait more than ten minutes and say it's okay when he arrives.
   c.   Leave right away.

Now there could be another outcome of the first sexual encounter: What if the sex wasn't good? There are so many possible causes, and a bad experience could awaken different reactions from different women: Maybe he was too excited to be with you. Maybe he's a selfish lover. Maybe he felt under pressure to "perform." Maybe it was you. Women will come up with endless reasons.

There are so many possible maybes in this scenario, but it all depends on exactly what happened. It also depends on what kind of personalities you two have. Maybe if you're not really passionate and he's a selfish lover, which could work for you, however strange it may sound. So giving any advice on this particular situation is very difficult, and you will have to decide according to circumstances and what is in your best interest.

ESTABLISHING YOURSELF AND YOUR EXPECTATIONS IN A RELATIONSHIP

CHAPTER 11

Developing the Relationship You Want

Developing the relationship you want is like raising a child in some ways. You as a parent decide many things in your children's development. You raise them; they don't raise you. You teach them how to be respectful to others and to you, and to be honest. And you do this by example—by the way you treat them, love them, nurture them, and, yes, punish them when necessary. All of that will influence and instill morals and values they will follow and that will guide them in their lives. You have the most influence and power, not their teachers, not their coaches, and not their friends. These people can help and provide positive influence, but ultimately it's your work that is more important.

Your relationship needs the same kind of attention, especially in the beginning. Love is not enough; you need the skills to do it right. Just as you need parenting skills, you need relationship skills. It's always easier to teach someone something new than to try to break a bad habit that he or she has already developed.

So even though you know what you want and you're pretty sure you have a man who shares your goals and interests, there is still quite a bit of work to be done. You want to create a lifestyle in which he treats you the way you want to be treated. I know you may ask why you have to do the work and not him. Well, he's doing the work. He's looking to satisfy his needs and his goals, so you'd better take care of yours. Believe me, even the man who loves you more than he loves himself will be lost and confused about what just happened when something goes wrong and you are upset. The bottom line is that we don't always know how, but if we love you, we will adjust to satisfy your needs and do things for you. We will help and do things we're told to do to keep the relationship fresh, exciting, and loving, but most likely we will not take initiative simply because we don't know how.

If you don't show us how to do that, one day we will wake up and just start thinking, *This is not what I want.* And the reason for our dilemma is going to be you. It's not going to be us. Not in our minds, anyway. When things start going bad, it's always the other person's fault. You will try to fix it, try to fix us, but the man will not try to fix you. He will start looking for something else, because he will not know how to fix things … how to change things. We don't see that your behavior may be the product of the way we have been treating you. For us it's simpler than that: it's simply you, and there's nothing we can do about it. Simply, we don't know what to do about it. The only thing left to do is to find some comfort, some satisfaction, or some excitement or whatever it is that we may be missing outside the home. Yes, I know it's wrong, but look around you; it's happening all the time. It's happening to people you know, and probably to some couples you thought were quite happy. Just saying that it's the wrong way to deal with problems and complaining about it will not make any difference. You can avoid all of that, but first you have to accept that it happens.

You have to accept that the power of change lies within you. You have to be the leading force in getting things back on the right track. Your lover/husband will follow, but he cannot lead, because he doesn't know how. And, yes, even he could be going through that situation right now. You have to focus on the result and the tactics to get through to him. Let me put it this way, if you wait for your husband to notice that the kitchen needs to be renovated and for him to take the initiative, and if you expect him to do it the way you like, you will be in for a long wait. (If you already have the kind of a man who will take the initiative and make you a perfect kitchen, you don't really need to read this book. But the other 99 percent of women should continue.)

Men are not wired to think that way. As I have said before, we provide and protect. You make a house a home. You nurture the children. Yes, we love them too, but a mother's love is special. That's why the courts give children to the mother in the majority of divorce cases unless she is really unfit to care for them. You're better at some things than we are, and we are better at other things.

If we don't show love the same way you do, that doesn't mean we don't love you. Your man might not be fulfilling your needs simply because he doesn't know how, and not because he doesn't want to. Maybe you're trying to explain it to him the way you would to your girlfriends. They seem to understand, but he doesn't, especially if you didn't train him from the beginning. I use the word *train* because many times you ladies refer to your husbands as one of your kids. You have to do for him as much as you do for them … then you might as well think in terms of training him. Just as you teach your kids to do certain things, you can teach him. Just as it's easier to teach the kids while they're young, it's easier to teach a man in the beginning of the relationship. It's easier to teach new habits than to break old ones.

When you start a relationship, you don't expect him to call you every day or text you or tell you where he is. And that's fine. You don't want to appear to be too possessive and jealous. The trick is to always do less than he does. Always leave it to him for the next phone call. When the date is finished, he should be asking for the next one. You just tell him to call you just to make sure. If he doesn't call for a while, don't wait for him. Don't be available. You didn't think he was going to call, so you made other plans. If he's surprised or disappointed, just ask, "Did you expect me to put my life on hold after a couple of dates? Did you expect me to wait around for your call?" If he wanted to see you, he shouldn't have waited so long, and next time he won't. If he's the right one, he will correct his mistake and if he's not, just let him go. Just think of it like this: if you're going away, you will probably book a hotel room a few days in advance, unless you're planning to stay in one of those roadside motels with rooms always available. Now is that what you think of yourself? A roadside motel? If not, you deserve a call from your man. Anything that is worth anything must be booked ahead.

So as the relationship develops, women tend to do more and more while men follow kind of reluctantly, as they're not eager to completely give up on the life they have. You need to be the one who does a little bit less. There should be less initiative on your part and more on his. This is how you set your standards. This is how you declare you want to be treated. You want to be persuaded. Don't be all his after three or four dates. You can still slip away out of his hands. If he shows up for a date late, you can accept it once if there's a really good reason. But not the second time—don't even bother answering the phone or opening the door. As a matter of fact you shouldn't even be at home. Go out. Go to your girlfriend's house. Just go. You're already dressed for a date. I don't care if it's his job, his mother, his friend, or anything else. Next time you speak with him, tell him not to arrange dates at times when he could be held up. If it's a crazy time at work, he should know that and explain it to you ahead of time. If he's driving his mother to the doctor, he should know there could be delays in the office or traffic on the way back. He should tell you that and let you make plans with your friends. He can always come join you later whenever he's finished. Thinking of you going out with your friends and being hit on will not be happy thoughts in his mind. He will try to avoid that situation any way he can. That means being on time. That is the balance of power. If he's on time, you're with him. If he's not, he has no right to tell you where to be. He should not keep you waiting at home. Being on time is the right way, and it's how he shows respect for you. Everything else is an excuse, and that's all there is—an excuse. And we know who we can use them on. For example, if you have a job you don't care about, and you can get a similar job the next day, how much do you care if you come to work late? On the other hand, if you love your job and you know your employer doesn't tolerate tardiness (because it is very disrespectful to everyone else who makes sure to be on time), how hard will you try never to be late? That's exactly what it is. Don't analyze it and twist it around, and don't let him do that to you. That's how men think and conduct themselves; we think black and white—is she worth it or not? So are you worth it?

When you're out on a date you should always feel like the most important person to him. If you don't, just drift away, and when he comes looking for you, tell him you didn't think he would notice you were gone. Tell him to go back and enjoy himself. Surely someone else will find you interesting enough to keep you company. If he's looking around or being too cute with the waitresses, you have to react. Be consistent. Even if he doesn't realize what he's doing, it still reflects badly on you, and he needs to learn. Don't start complaining to him. Men consider that nagging. He will try to convince you that you're crazy. Give him the cold shoulder. A little flirting with someone else on your part will get the message across much better than a thousand words could explain.

Remember, everything he can do, you can do better. Don't get loud. There's no point to it. We understand actions better than words. If he's not holding the door for you, if he's talking on his cell phone rather than to you, or doing anything that shows that you are not a priority, or anything that you find disrespectful, you have to react. If he walks in front of you, just stop. Let him come back and then ask him, "Is there someone here that you wouldn't want seeing us together? Am I your sidekick who is supposed to walk in your shadow?" When he talks on his cell phone for too long, go talk to someone else, and don't come back when he's finished. If he's all in with his buddies joking and laughing and leaving you out, just step away. Someone will come to talk to you. When your man comes for you, tell him not to worry. Tell him to have fun. You're capable of finding your ride home. Trust me, you won't have to do this twice, but you will have to do it at some point if you want the respect you deserve.

He will learn really fast. We are good at adapting and learning what kind of woman we have on our arms and how we have to treat her if we want to keep her. A woman with standards makes a man feel more important. And I'm not talking a high-maintenance sort of woman. I'm talking about a woman who knows what she has to offer and demands complementary respect and behavior from her man. This is a woman most men could not have. We like to feel that you have chosen us to court you; we didn't just pick you up. A lot of men can pick up chicks, but when we find that someone special is interested in us, that means we must be special also. These are the fundamentals of a relationship to be cherished and respected by both sides. That is why you will get everything back from a good man that you put in. There are a lot of good men out there, and you can have one of them, but you can also ruin him by letting him walk all over you. Once you establish a relationship like this, there will be no need for effort to continue on that path. It will be a way of life, a lifestyle that you will both live. And he will need a little kick in the butt, a little reminder from time to time, because men don't naturally think that way. As long as you don't let it go for too long and you stay consistent, you will have a respectful and loving man.

There is a stick and carrot strategy in a relationship. The stick was him needing to be put in place. Now the carrot is just as important— the reward is just as much of a motivator as punishment, as long as you keep the balance. The reward is what separates you from being a woman with standards and being a high-maintenance woman. As I keep saying, we are the hunters; you are the prey. You don't want to be easy prey; we don't want that either. It's your requirements that make you worthy prey and gives us a feeling of accomplishment. Now there's a difference between being worthy prey and being difficult. Worthy prey balances between the carrot and the stick. You make demands, but you give certain things in return. High maintenance is just that—too much effort for too little reward.

The way you show your man appreciation for the things he does for you is very important, and in the beginning you will have to demand that he does those things. Of course you shouldn't have to demand or ask for anything; he should know on his own. Well, he doesn't, and don't expect him to. Remember, we think differently. But if you give him a little time, if you train him, he will learn.

Men will adjust. We are very aware that getting a carrot is much better than getting a stick, so even though you have to teach him, you still need to recognize his actions. Don't think his actions are less worthy because you had to tell him, and he didn't think of it himself first. It doesn't mean he never thinks of you first. So just recognize his actions, say, "Thank you, love," give him a smile, give him a kiss. If he takes you somewhere you've never been or you see he really thought about the outing and tried to take you somewhere he thought you would like, thank him for his thoughtfulness. Tell him you enjoyed it even if it wasn't that great. Find something good to say about it. There will be a lot of time later to let him know that it was fun once, but it's not really your kind of place.

So remember a few things: Make him feel special but not essential. Don't start asking for the next date; let him do it. Always do a little bit less than he does. Use actions instead of words, because everything we do you can do better. Be worthy and not difficult. Recognize his effort even if you have to remind him from time to time. Accept that we are wired differently from the way you are, and don't dwell on it. Be consistent in your demands; don't make us figure out what you're thinking, because you will be disappointed. We see black, white, red, blue, and green. We don't see fuchsia or vermillion or midnight blue. That's for you and your girlfriends. With your man keep it simple. You have the power, and we will adjust.

CHAPTER 12

How to Keep Your Man

There are two ways of thinking about how to keep your man, or how to treat your man in a relationship. The first way is exemplified by the wives' tales that says that a woman needs to do so much for a man, because men are men and you can't change them. Men want a woman with three hats. First, they want a chef in the kitchen, which means a woman to feed them. As they say, the way to a man's heart is through his stomach. Second, they want a classy lady to show off in public—a woman they would be proud to have on their arm … a sophisticated woman, nicely dressed, desired by many but only his to have. Third, they want a call girl in the bedroom. Yes, I know I can imagine your sarcastic response as you are reading this. I'm sorry about that, but maybe if God created women first she could have told him how to make a man. It did not work out that way, so this is the reality you have now.

It's not all bad news; there is some good. You don't have to be perfect at all of this, just good. Seriously, we can help with the first one, and we can eat take out from time to time. The second one is not so hard either. Most women love to dress nicely and wear makeup. By dressing up and going out for dinner, you are wearing your #1 and #2 hat. The third hat needs a little explanation—something that you probably never thought of and something you are probably a little uncomfortable with. Men sometimes feel uneasy doing all the things they want to in bed with the mother of their children, so a woman has to make him know that she's still a wife, and not just a mother, so he can express his sexual side more openly. Single men will brag about the sex they have. Men will even brag about sex with their mistresses. But most men are reluctant to talk with other men about the sex they have with their wives. It is a funny taboo for a man. That is the mother of his children. He makes love to her. Treating her like a sex object makes many men uncomfortable. So don't just say, "I don't want our sex life to be routine." Don't ask your man if he's satisfied with it. Tell him you want to try something new, but you're embarrassed to talk about it. Don't tell him right away what it is. Make him guess; it will make you feel a little bit more comfortable if he also opens up. Make it a game. That way, little by little, you will both be more open and have more fun. Always remember that you are a wife and a woman to your man, and make sure he sees you as that and not just the mother of his children.

The second theory about how to keep a man is supported by women whom men like to call feminists. They always fight over anything they feel they "must" do for a man; they always question why they have to do anything. Why doesn't the man do it first? They care about keeping an even score more than anything else; even if it doesn't take any effort, they won't do something if it's not their turn. Being equal doesn't mean we do the exact same things for each other. It doesn't mean we share the same responsibilities and chores fifty-fifty. It doesn't mean that, if the man changed the tire last time, you should do it next time. If he opened the door for you yesterday, you will have to do it for him today (and, yes, I know you can open your own door). "Down with all the chivalry and the world would be a better place?" I know these are extreme examples, but some women do take this sort of "equality" all the way down to the basics of everyday life.

I'm not saying that men are not capable of doing laundry or aren't supposed to do laundry—or vacuum, cook, or help with the children. All I'm saying is that we, as men and women, have different needs. Even women themselves appreciate different kinds of help from their men. Some women want a man to take care of the kids for a day so they can do something they have to do. Some women may want the men to stay at home and do things with them.

Being equal partners isn't about being equal—fifty-fifty—in everyday life. It's about fulfilling our needs whatever they may be. If the man cannot cook, why eat a well screwed up meal every second day when he's good at cleaning the kitchen after dinner? If he doesn't clean the house "correctly," perhaps he can do the laundry. It's all about a balance that you can find with your partner. It's about doing the chores we are best at. My friend Mike had never cooked a meal in his life. When he moved from his parents' home into his first apartment, he invited us for a few drinks. He bought a frozen pizza at the grocery store. Good thing we were all drinking, so we didn't notice he put the pizza in the oven still wrapped in the plastic. We figured it out later when we found the sticker on the bottom of one of the slices. He would walk downstairs from his apartment and cross the street to buy a cup of coffee and walk all the way back before he would make it at home. When he married, asking him to cook would be a disaster. But Mike was a whiz at cleaning the kitchen. He would wash the floors every couple of months down on his knees with a brush and disinfectant. Mike did laundry all the time, but he never took the children to the doctors; he couldn't watch them cry when they were getting their shots. But Mike's wife never gave the kids their baths; Mike always did. Now I don't know how much of an even score that was, but they were pretty equal partners. Neither of them kept track of who did what on Monday or Wednesday or Friday. They just automatically complemented each other and didn't keep score. Did she do a little bit more? Did he? I don't know, but they divided chores by their strengths and abilities, and it worked for them and still does.

So you need to have a balance. Don't be a doormat and do everything for your husband and even your kids. On the other hand, don't try to make a point by making everything fifty-fifty. We're all better at one or two things than we are at others. Being equal partners means sharing responsibilities and chores according to the best way for things to be done. That will also give you free time to enjoy each other, enjoy the family time, and have some time for yourself.

If you want your man to participate in these activities, you will have to do your part. Remember the basic needs we talked about in the beginning? Men want to be your heroes. We are providers, protectors, and of course we are always horny. So if our primary needs are satisfied, we will participate. Before you got married, you satisfied your man all the time so why not now? Yes, I know you have no time, you're tired, and if he helped more you would be more willing. The man says he would help more if there was a reward at the end. It's a circle you have to break. It will have to come from you. Think of it this way: all men are dogs (sound familiar?). Would you starve your dog for three or four days and then try to train him? He wouldn't be too eager to follow your instructions. He would be thinking only about filling his stomach.

Again, it's about the carrot and the stick: provide a reward for good deeds, and take away something he likes for bad deeds. You will have to use a little bit of skill when you are depriving your man of something; a grown man doesn't want to be treated like a child, but as long as he gets the message that rewards are up to him, he will oblige.

I know you want to say—why doesn't he do something first? Then you will reward him. Well, it doesn't work that way. Men don't look to figure out how to make the relationship they're in work better. Men look to fulfill their needs. We don't hear you complaining; all we hear is nagging. We don't hear that you are tired, that you don't have time for anything; we just hear excuses. We go to work too. We see ourselves busy all day long and feel that our job is harder than yours, but we still manage to do it. We don't see that your day is as busy as ours; we see you as unorganized, spoiled, and exaggerating. However you look at it, it all sounds like nagging to us. We don't organize the life inside the home. We don't decorate the home. We don't plan the daily routines. It's not in our DNA. It's just not, and there is no vaccine for it. We will not take the lead. We will get a big-screen TV and a garage or maybe a basement for a "man cave," and that's it. That's all we need, and we are happy with it. You don't care what kind of engine we have in the car or what kind of tools we have in the shed. You don't care about those kinds of things, and we don't care about house chores.

If we ask you for help with something—putting up a shelf or organizing something—you do it, but we will not get mad because you didn't take the initiative to do so. Why do you get mad when we don't take the initiative? We tell you exactly what we want you to do. We don't make you read our minds to figure out what we want. Men don't want to worry about planning and organizing things inside the home, but that doesn't mean we can't do these tasks if we are told to. Make it simple and we will do our part. Give us some chores that we can do, and we will do them. Don't give us ten rules for doing laundry with seven different detergents, softeners, and machine cycles. We can do white, dark, regular, and delicate. We can clean the house if you don't have different procedures for every piece of wood in the house, different products for every piece of furniture, and multiple carpet cleaners and tile disinfectants. Give us tools and materials, show us how, and don't make it sound more complicated than brain surgery.

So, if you're focused on achieving the goal more than getting it done your way, your man will do a good job. Men are goal oriented. We want to get the job done and move on. Let's not talk about it. Let's not discuss what we should do first. Should we clean now or after the upcoming party that we are having? What will people say if something is not clean? But then again, we will have to do it again after the party, and there are other things that may need to be done first. No I'm already tired of housework. Make it simple. What do you want me to do? Don't involve your man in the process that goes through your mind. Just give him his chores. Show him how, let him organize himself, and it will be done.

If you communicate with your man in the language he understands, you will get the help and you will find some extra time for yourself and for the two of you. It will be pretty much the same when it comes to organizing your quality time with your husband and your family. If you share your chores around the house with your husband and kids, you will have some time left to spend it together. Your kids are never too young to pick up their toys or clean their room, and your husband is never too old to start helping out. If you don't organize the time to do something together, if you don't start first, they will end up in front of the TV or the computer while you end up doing everything by yourself. You can pick some games to play, and after a couple of times you can tell the kids, "Next time Dad will bring you a new game to try." Now, you will have to remind him, but do it in a way that shows you are excited to see what he's going to bring. Don't give him a lecture about how he's already forgotten about it. If you go to the mall, take him with you and send him to the toy store while you do some other shopping. That will keep him from having to be irritated waiting for you in every store you go in, and he will already be in the mall, so he might as well go and find something to play. Afterward, you two can grab coffee or lunch and spend some time together. You can even use lunch as an excuse to go to the mall, and while you're there you might as well pick up a couple of things. Your time for just the two of you will depend on your initiative and reminding him of his participation or his turn to surprise you. It will depend on your excitement about it and not your negative comments. Don't let him forget about his part. Don't give him a lecture. Don't set him up to fail, because he will.

Vacations will work better if you organize them. Put money aside and take control. He will be happy that you did. So there is a way you can get a lot of help from your husband if you give him the information in a way that he can process and apply it. As the old saying goes, he might be the head of the family, but you're the neck. Wherever the neck turns, the head will follow, and you can have all your needs and requirements fulfilled without taking his fangs out. He still needs to feel like a man, like a provider and protector of the family. He needs to have purpose and a role in the household, because if he doesn't he won't be good to anyone. Remember, unhappy men don't try to figure out how to fix the things that are wrong in the home. They don't know how to make a relationship work. They really don't know what to do, so they start feeling trapped, and they look for a temporary escape from reality. They look for instant gratification outside their home to fulfill their needs. If they're disconnected from you and the role they are supposed to play, they feel no sense of purpose, so what difference does it make what they do? Thinking and feeling that way never ends well. Let your man be a man. Be a smart woman. If you don't insist on things to be done "your way or the high way," if you apply a little strategy and accept that we operate differently, you can have a real loving and respectful relationship. The mother in the movie *My Big Fat Greek Wedding* believes that, if you make him think it was his idea, he'll do anything. Honey always gets more bees than vinegar.

CHAPTER 13

Why Men Cheat

Now that's a million-dollar question that seems to come with a million different answers. Every therapist, every survey comes up with new theories and many different versions of similar answers. The problem is that everybody tries to figure out what makes men cheat and the reasons for cheating rather than why it is easier for men to cheat than it is for women.

Once you understand why men are capable of cheating, you will know how to prevent it. Remember, you have the power. First you need to understand—actually you don't need to understand, you just need to accept it—men need sex. As I said before, it's a need just like you have the need to bear children. It's just as strong as a maternal need to nurse them, to take care of them, and make a home for them. Don't question it. You as a woman don't know better than a man does about his own needs. No, you really don't. So just accept it that it's just as strong as your need. It really makes no difference that your needs are more noble and honorable and moral. A need is a need, so accept it as that. Don't compare his sexual need to your shopping or decorating the house or gardening interests. Those are just hobbies like golfing, fishing, and hunting. Again, more times than not everybody benefits from your hobbies, and only a man benefits from his. But sex is not a hobby; it's a need, and you have to accept it as that. The sooner you do, the less likely you are to become another statistic. Now, the reasons for cheating fall under three general categories:

- To fulfill a physical need
- To build ego in the hunter (power trip)
- To respond to something that has gone really wrong at home

First, let's look at cheating to fulfill a physical need. Lots of surveys ask men if they cheated and why. Most of the answers come back along the same lines: "I was feeling disconnected from my wife. I never felt good enough. Nothing I did seemed to be good enough. We drifted apart." So someone takes a survey by shoving a microphone in a guys' face, asking him questions, and expecting the complete truth. Nobody wants to look like an ass. You may think, *Why would they care? They don't know the people asking those questions; they are strangers to them.* Let me ask you this—do you care about picking your nose in front of a stranger? If you answered yes, then why? You will never see that person again. Simply, you don't want to look like an ass, and no one else does either.

Let's try to do an experimental survey. Send a pretty woman to ask the questions. Do you have a small penis? I'm sure that's another subject men don't care to lie about. The next thing is, someone puts this poor soul on national TV on some talk show with his wife of twenty years in front of millions of people. I'm sure his family will be watching, and so will hers, and their kids and probably most of their friends and neighbors too. Obviously there is no pressure to lie and try to make yourself less of an ass now that you've already been caught. He cares what his family and friends think of him. He doesn't want to leave his wife and break up the family. He has to do damage control. I wonder what would happen if he said, "She was a gorgeous twenty-five-year-old with a great body, tight skin, firm breasts, and a perky ass. I was so turned on by it I just couldn't help it"? I'm sure that would go really well. It leaves a lot of room for reconciliation. Now there is another idea. He can try the emotional road about feeling disconnected from his wife. They stopped doing things together. He wasn't feeling like the man of the house. Now in this second scenario, there is something his wife can work with. It seems to be that the situation could have been avoided. She feels a little responsibility. Maybe it was her negligence that pushed him that way. Maybe if she started paying more attention to him and they could spend some time together making him feel good about himself, they could fix this together. She gets to keep the family together, saves the relationship and marriage, and she won't look as if he made a total fool of her. She will be seen as a forgiving woman in control. He's so remorseful and sorry that he will never do it again, and they can move on from it and be happy. She feels that she has power in her hands, that she can prevent this from happening again, and that he's not just being a dog but a man who made a mistake.

Now what would her options be if he gave answer number one. How would she be able to compete with a young girl? She can't go back in time. She can't look as she did when they got married, and even if she could it would not make a difference. If all that it takes is an attractive body for him to cheat, that temptation will always be around no matter what. That is why this answer will never come up even though it's the truth many times. How do I know? It's very simple. Open up the newspapers and open your eyes. Go online, watch TV and late-night commercials. Every day there are more and more escort services popping up. There are rub-and-tug massage parlors in every city. Now who do you think makes these businesses boom? Do you think it's the young ones? Students with all the money left over from their tuition fees? Or maybe men who are in the work force already starting with a $20,000 per year salary? Young guys prefer going to the bars, having fun partying, and finding and getting it for free. There are not enough rich boys to keep all those places open all over the world. When your man goes there, do you really think there is some sort of sociology or marriage counseling diploma hanging on the wall above the masseuse's bed?

Do you really think they are sharing feelings, and he just needs to feel connected and cared for by another woman? Maybe it's time to wake up and read the signs. Listen to the logic and not what you want to hear. You know who keeps these businesses open, and they will stay open because most women don't know how to make sure that a man lying beside them is not the one keeping them busy. Oh I know you hope it's not your man, and you really don't want to believe it is, but you should make sure that it's not. If you want to hope, hope for good weather. Your relationship won't become wonderful just because that's what you hope for. It will only become wonderful if you use your power to make it that way.

Second, is he cheating to build ego in the hunter? This is the ultimate power trip. Men are hunters; they need the thrill of the hunt and the satisfaction of accomplishment. We need to achieve this in one form or another. I know you are thinking, *What kind of accomplishment is sex? It's disgusting … just like an animal.* I guess that's why they call men dogs. Please don't try to understand it. Don't analyze it with your girlfriends; they don't know any better than you do. I'm going to repeat it again and again—accept that's the way it is. Accept that that's how we are wired. Only then you can eliminate it.

They say everything's fair in love and war. Well, in war the better you know your enemy, the better your chance of defeating him. Same goes for love—the better you know your spouse, the better your chance of keeping him straight. The best thing your girlfriend can tell you that he's a pig, he doesn't deserve you, and you're so much better than he. This might be comforting for a moment, but it will make no difference. Now, as I said, men are driven by accomplishment. Even men who are successful in their respective fields have an urge to do something to distinguish themselves from others. Men spend most of their time around people who are at their own social level. If he is the successful CEO of some big company, most likely the men around him are in similar fields and are successful. So there is nothing really distinguishing him and his accomplishments from them and theirs. If he works construction, the people around him are in the construction business and are also more or less as good at what they do as he is. Most men talk about some glory days, something they did in the past, something that will make other people admire them, think they are cool. This feeds their egos. Most men will say they have a great wife, a great family. They'll say they're lucky, but that is a two-minute conversation. He can talk for a long time about some high school football game that made him a star, or something unique and crazy that he did in the past. Those are the things that define us as men, the things that separate us from all the guys around us that do the same thing we do. Those accomplishments make us feel special ... make us feel envied by others. We feel superior in that small world around us. It's the little goals, the little achievements, the little things that we can do, but others around us can't. It's the challenge, the competition, and the ego that pushes us to show that we are still capable of doing something others can't. It doesn't matter what we do, how powerful or rich we are, there are always people around us, or who came before us, whom we are competing with.

Now it may sound trivial to you, but persuading and winning another woman will also feel like an accomplishment that will separate him from the pack. He's still capable of achieving things that his friends cannot. He's more than just a plumber, or a lawyer, or a CEO like his friends and counterparts. His ego is getting fed, and the legend in his own mind lives on. Being able to pursue and conquer other women is a big part of a man's ego. Men can admit to not being good in many fields. No man is embarrassed that he can't cook or sing or isn't good at certain sports, but they never say they aren't good lovers. That would be a very hard thing to accept. It's in the core of our being, and there is no measurement to say if we are good at it or not, so the only way to know is to be reassured by a woman, and the more reassurance a man gets, the better his ego feels.

Women don't talk about the glory days. They don't talk about cheerleading days or playing sports or any kind of recognition they received in their past. They may mention such achievements, but they don't dwell on them. Instead, they discuss their children or what they did for them, sometimes something stupid their husbands did, or some improvements in their homes. They'll talk about interactions within the family. They are relationship oriented. Men, on the other hand, are all about achievements and competition. That's why we like sports, hunting, fishing, or anything else that is competitive— anything that involves winning or beating the odds.

I will say it again: you women are better people. You have higher morals and values, but that will not help you. It's like walking into a lion's cage. You think he's not hungry, and you believe that he knows you won't hurt him. You believe he won't hurt you because you feed him four times a day and you're nice to him. Well, I don't think you would take that chance, but you seem to believe that, because a man said his vows when he married you, because he told you he loved you, he will be faithful to you and take care of you and not hurt you. You hope all his ego-controlled needs will just disappear because you are so good to him. There are women who have good husbands, but they are good husbands because their wives didn't leave it to chance. They understood men and how they operate better than other women, and they have taken control.

Third, some men cheat because something has gone wrong at home. Now that is the easiest one to avoid if you love your man and care for him. When you love someone, the things you do for him don't feel like chores, because you want to do them. Make him feel important, because he wants to be your hero. We want to feel we are providing for and protecting the family. Yes, we don't want to talk about it, but we do like a little recognition. We need you to show us we are still number one from time to time. I know you want to hear those things too, but we aren't talking about you right now. You don't need to be kept in line, so listen up. You will always have a purposeful role in the family. On the other hand, our roles in a conventional sense get smaller and smaller. We are usually not the sole provider anymore, and as we get older the importance of our roles seems to diminish even more. As we get older we need you more than you need us, and the kids still need a mother more than a father as they grow up. So if a man doesn't feel like a protector and provider of the family, he starts to question his self-worth. If he doesn't feel that you will come to him when things get bad and that you don't have faith in him that he can fix things, it will be devastating to his ego. So what difference does it make what he does when no one needs him anymore anyway?

Ego is a great motivator, but it can also be our downfall. It can propel us to do great things, but it can also steer us in the wrong direction. Losing our self-worth and our confidence that we can be what we are expected to be—by ourselves and others—will take a man down the wrong path. He still needs to feel as if he's your hero. If he does, he will be much better to you. Don't destroy his self-worth if he's down on his luck. Don't take the fangs out of the dog and send him out into the wild.

Now we have explored the basic categories into which millions of different reasons for cheating fall. Any reason—and there are more than you can think of—will fit into one of these three basic categories.

As I said in the beginning, there are reasons that men cheat. But another question to ask is why are men so much more capable of cheating than women? The answer is very simple: men can separate sex and love. That is all there is to it. That is your answer, and I will explain it. I'm sure you've heard the line, "I had sex with her, but I make love to you." You think that's such a pile of garbage, but men really believe that and feel that way. We can have sex without love, and we can have sex with one woman while we are in love with another woman. For example, two men can be great friends, go out for drinks, have fun, party, and have a great time, but tomorrow when they go to work and one of them is the boss, he will have no problem reaming the other one out if he doesn't perform. It's different—work is work. One of them is the boss, and the other one needs to do his job. But after work they're friends again. At work we wear different hats than we do in private, and men accept that. That's how it is and how it should be. The job has to be taken care of. We can be best friends or just coworkers, but we don't mix work with personal life.

Women, on the other hand, would get upset over that same situation. She wouldn't be able to understand how they could have had such a good time last night, and now she's being criticized by her boss, the woman she'd just been socializing with. Everything is personal with women.

So it's the same principle with men when it comes to sex and making love. We can separate sex and love. One has nothing to do with the other. And I know you can't understand it, but as I said, you don't have to understand it. Just accept it.

That is how we think, but that is where the power of change lies. That is one thing that you have to change in his mind—you have to make him see how wrong it is to be with another woman. You have to make him see how much he would hurt you, how much he would disappoint you. Make him understand that he won't be your hero anymore, he won't be that special man that he needed to be to get a woman like you on his arm. He would be just another statistic, not worth the love, affection, and respect that you are used to giving him. You have to explain to him that his roles as man of the house would be compromised in your eyes. He needs to understand that it's never "just sex." If he is unfaithful, everything will change in your eyes. That single act will completely change your perception of him as a man. His values, morals, and character will stand for nothing in your mind. It's not just a physical need or ego thing that he's fulfilling; it's an act of disrespect to you and what you two have together. It's a devaluation of his role as a man that you would go to when things get bad, the provider and the protector of the family unity that he is supposed to serve. The unity that is supposed to be protected by him is broken apart by that single act. He needs to understand the impact of that betrayal; he needs to understand the pain he would cause you. Once he understands that, no reason or temptation will be worth it or strong enough to lure him to look for a solution to his problems outside of the marriage.

So don't try to analyze all the different reasons that men cheat. Instead, look to disable that primal part of his brain that makes him think it's "just sex." It never is for you, so it shouldn't be for him either.

CHAPTER 14

Fixing your Relationship

How do you fix and change a problem that has been going on for a long time? You've been taken for granted and not appreciated for years by your husband. You feel like a maid and a servant in your own home rather than the wife and equal partner that you started out to be. You have put everyone and everything ahead of yourself and your needs. It seems as if you keep giving to your husband and kids and really getting no help or acknowledgement back from them.

Women fall into that trap, and the whole purpose of their lives turns out to be nurturing the children, taking care of the house, the husband, and everything else but themselves. As we talked about before, you will be treated as you demand to be treated. The change has to start with you. It's human nature to take advantage of others, even when we love them. Your situation is not unique and neither is the solution, but you will have to be the one who makes the change. If you haven't taught your kids to help out, don't expect them to say, "Mom, I'll do my own laundry so you can get some time to yourself." Likewise, your husband will not get up from watching sports on TV and say, "Honey, let me cook today so you can go out for a few hours and do something for yourself." If you clean and cook for them all the time, they will not offer to do those things on their own. Maybe they'll help out on your birthday or Mother's Day, but not on a regular basis. Why would they? You don't enjoy doing the chores, and neither will they. They believe it's your job anyway, and they easily get used to having everything done for them.

They're not bad kids; they just have bad habits—instilled in them by you. They didn't come out of your womb trained like that, and neither did your husband. I bet on your first couple of dates your husband didn't tell you, "Listen, woman, when we marry you will cook and clean and do all the chores. I'm not planning on helping you with anything." If he did say that and you still married him, then I can't help you. When your kids have everything done for them, they won't be rushing to move out. You will be expected to service them forever. When they have their own kids, you'll do everything for them all over again, and you will be expected to. That's why kids stay at home these days into their thirties. Why would they move away from free rent, a free maid, and a cook? They'd be crazy to leave. You might be fulfilling the nurturing side of yourself to such an extent that you are providing more than your family's needs. You're not doing them a favor; you're just crippling them—and yourself—for life.

What potential wife will do for your son what you do right now? What man will want to be a servant to your daughter who can't do anything around the house? Kids are never too young to have some chores, and they will never be too old to stop taking advantage of you. They need to grow up, and so do you. You have to recognize the difference between the need and the convenience. When they get older, most of the time they don't need you, but it's very convenient for them to have you around. And all that applies to your husband just as much.

The first thing we have to talk about is fixing *you*. Once you accomplish that, everything else will fall into place. It's your fault. I will repeat: it is your fault. Your behavior allowed all this to happen. You created the situation you're living in, and only you have the power to change it. The most important part of this lesson is "you have the power"! If you don't believe that, you won't be able to change anything.

Your kids and husband will fight you and complain once you start making changes. That's normal; nobody in his or her right mind would give up all that pampering without resistance. They will hope it's just a phase you're going through. Maybe you're just pissed off and will complain for a few days, and then it will all go away, and things will be back to normal. You have to stay on track even when they're calling you a bad mother and a bad wife. Sooner or later they will adjust. They will respect you more in the end.

You have to decide to change your ways. You have to decide to change your lifestyle. You can't fake it. Don't say, "I'll do it for a month and see what happens." This change must be for good. Life is too short, and there's no going back. You have served your kids and your husband for a long time—five years, ten, or twenty. It doesn't matter. You have to get some of that "me time" back. You will be happier and so will your husband and kids once they adjust. You won't be nagging them and complaining about everything you have to do and how no one is helping you. Family members will not go out of their way to take some of the load off your back until it affects them. It will not happen. They way you're doing things is not working, so you have to change your approach; you have to change your ways. If you get on the road that leads to Los Angeles, that is where you will end up. You can complain and whine and curse, but it won't do you any good. You can wish and pray to be on the road to New York, but as long as you don't take a different road, you're going to end up in LA. So you have to get off that road, you have to change your way and get on the right road that will get you where you want to go.

Complaining about the situation will not do anything. You don't even have to know that you're on the right path, but you have to realize that what you've been doing so far is not working. Doing the same thing over and over again will not change the result no matter how much you hope it will, so it's up to you to make a change, and it will work whether you're a young family or a retired couple. Children and husbands are capable of helping; they just find it easier when you do your usual good job and they don't have to contribute. Change may seem easier for younger families, because younger kids and husbands may find it easier to adjust to change. Younger kids are more dependent on their moms, but they are easier to train. On the other hand, younger families are busier with more challenges and responsibilities than an older couple. Older couples are more set in their ways, but older husbands need their wives much more than grown kids do.

Let's take a look at typical young family situations. It's very easy to get caught up in everyday challenges—paying the bills, raising kids, pursuing careers. Husband and wife both work hard, but if you wait to have fun until you have enough money and the kids are grown, you will miss out on many years of life together. These are years that you can't get back. These are the years that you will remember as filled only with struggle, work, and challenge.

You have to prioritize the things in your life to find time for actual living. Your children will survive if you are not constantly there, but your marriage won't survive if you and your husband don't find time for yourselves. Don't turn into "just a mother." You're still a woman and a wife. You need to stay a woman to your husband. You need to be attractive to him. You need to remember all the reasons he married you. I know you have needs too, but first we'll talk about you, and then we'll talk about how you can get from him all the things you need. Trust me, unless his needs are satisfied, he will not worry about yours. He will not put your needs before his, so let's see how you can satisfy his needs. After that, there will be no problem in taking care of yours.

That's where your leverage is. If you're giving him nothing, he has nothing to lose. Why would he bother to add some of your daily load to his own load? Don't start going all noble on me with ideas that family should be first and all that. A man will satisfy his needs; he will make time for that. Remember, we are not wired the same as women. So think about what made him approach you the first time, and what made him fall in love with you. If those things have dramatically changed, why do you think his feelings won't have changed? If what he loved about you is gone, what is there to love? And you know what will happen next—you will become a statistic. So remember, there is a time to be a mother, but there has to be time to be a wife, and especially a time to be a woman.

If you think he will understand all the reasons you have for not being able to satisfy his needs, you are wrong. His needs need to be fulfilled; that's the bottom line. If you let yourself go, you have to fix yourself up. If you put on ten to fifteen pounds after having children, it won't matter. You will still be attractive. You will still be able to do the things you did before. You will still be able to participate in things that you've done for fun before. Feel good about yourself, and be confident. Your personality will be the same, and you will be the woman that he married. If you put on thirty to forty pounds, "Houston we have a problem."

It will make a difference to him. Ask yourself, if you had been this size when you met, would he have approached you? It doesn't matter—read again: it doesn't matter—to him that you have popped out three of his children. It does not matter. We see other women who have come back from childbirth, so everything you say—all your reasons—are just excuses to us. Believe me, he may not be telling you, but that's what he's thinking. Also your attitude will change with additional weight. You probably won't be able to do things you did before. You won't even have the desire to do them. You might not feel comfortable going to the beach, dressing up, going out, or participating in activities that you used to do. It all becomes a challenge to you. Now, he either has to give up doing these things with you, or he will continue doing them on his own, which will take away your time together. You stay home cleaning, and he goes out skiing. He won't give up what he likes to do, but when he comes home he will hear about your busy day and everything you had to do while he was out having fun. If he does give up what he likes to do, he will resent you. You may want to believe there's a third option to this that would be more favorable to you, but there isn't. Remember the reasons that made him approach you the first time and fall in love with you? There will be less time to do things you did together before, but you won't lose him completely. He loves you. He connects with you, but he's a much more a visual person than you are. A man doesn't want to have sex with the mother of his children. He doesn't want to have sex with any mothers; he wants to have sex with a woman—the one he chose. The one he wanted to marry and spend his life with. So keep those things alive, physically and emotionally.

It will be up to you to keep the fire going. It will have to be your initiative, and he will follow your lead. He needs to be told what is expected of him. He will do it, but don't make him read your mind. Remember, men are always the first ones to look for some gratification or fulfillment outside the marriage rather than trying to fix the relationship, because simply we don't know how. You will have to organize those "just the two of you" nights. Do something special for the two of you—a romantic surprise dinnertime alone, and of course some fun after dessert. Then you can tell him how much you would really love for him to plan the next outing. Maybe he could organize something for one night next month. Don't say it's "his turn" to do it, or that he owes you one. Don't make it a chore. Just show him how excited you are about it … how happy he will make you.

A man wants to be your hero and not to be nagged into doing something. Yes, you will have to remind him, but do it by showing excitement. Tell him you can't wait to see what he's planned. Don't say you know he's already forgotten about it and tell him he doesn't care. He may need a little reminder, but that doesn't mean he doesn't love you. Make sure he knows that the most important thing for you is to be together, just the two of you. There's no need for a big expense if you can't afford it.

When it comes to vacations you will have to organize them and put aside money to cover the expenses. Even if it's just a day trip with the kids, anything that will get you out of the everyday routine is a good idea. You want to break the routine that finds both of you at the end of the day too tired to do anything.

I know your daily load is huge. I understand that, but you have to distinguish between what is important and what can wait. You have to find a way to get help from him and from your kids if they are old enough. You should even ask for help from your family or friends for babysitting. Your children don't need you all the time. Women have been having children for thousands of years, and the needs of yours are no different from the needs of all the others. Wanting some time away from them doesn't mean that you don't love them. It doesn't mean that you're a bad mother if you get someone to babysit once a week. They will not get sick if they don't get a homemade meal from scratch every day. You don't have to prepare a different meal if they don't like the one you made in the first place. They can have lunch snacks for school from time to time or get a meal in the school cafeteria. They don't need designer clothes. Often they don't care even if you do, because you want people to say how cute they are. They won't care about clothes until they are teenagers. They don't need to sleep in your bed or your bedroom when they are babies or toddlers. Your room and your bed are for you and your husband. You have to stop overcompensating for your kids. Don't prepare the road for your kids; rather, prepare the kids for the road, and don't smother them with your love. Take care of their needs, but don't try to take away all the inconveniences; you won't be able to always be there for them.

There's always time to be made for you and your husband if you relegate the work and make some time for yourself. Don't feel that you have to prepare a big meal every day. Get your husband to clean up the kitchen while you put the kids to bed. Organize the chores so you two can have some time for yourselves at the end of the day. Stop putting so much responsibility on yourself, and get some help from your husband. He will be happy to do it if he knows you won't be so tired later on. Those are the times that should keep your marriage together—and not because you have kids together or you can't afford to get divorced, or you're afraid to end up alone.

There's nothing sweeter than when your man says, "Life is not always easy, but I would marry you all over again in a heartbeat." (And he's not saying it because you asked him to.) Your husband will be willing to help if he's told when and what—and of course he's looking for a little loving at the end of the day. Why not? It was a big part of your life before all the chores and responsibilities came along.

You also have to make some time for yourself. You're still a young woman. You still have girlfriends, some married, some single. Go out for lunch with them. Do some shopping—even window-shopping if money is tight. Go to a movie on the cheap night … whatever it is that interests you. You have to socialize with people outside the home. Don't worry, your hubby will watch the kids. He knows that you'll be coming home happy, feeling good with your batteries recharged, and when you're happy you won't be too tired to make him happy. He'll even offer to watch the kids, so stop trying to do everything yourself. You're allowed to have a life and to enjoy living, even when you have kids. When mama is happy, the whole house is happy … everybody gets what he or she needs.

When you have a family your priorities change, and that means that some things get done before others. It doesn't mean the other things don't need to be done at all. You have to make a balance in your life. You can't be 100 percent about the kids, the house, and the responsibility. Try 70 percent for kids and chores, 20 percent for you and your husband, and 10 percent for yourself. I know it's not fair that so much is put on you and you're trying to make everyone happy, but you have to take care of yourself. If you're on a boat that's sinking, the captain will tell you to put a life vest on yourself first, and then put them on your kids. It's the same with oxygen masks on a plane. This doesn't mean that you're putting yourself ahead of your kids. It means that if you don't survive, you can't help anyone else. If you're not happy, how can you make other people in your home happy? You take the lead, and your man will follow. He doesn't know how to lead; he's not wired that way. We provide and protect, so when we get home we feel as if our job is pretty much done. You can nag and complain about it, or you can take action that will benefit everyone. Don't think that saying, "We have to talk" will change anything. Change your approach, and your man will change with you.

Now let's look at an older couple whose children are older. Many things that apply to a younger couple still apply to you simply because of the relationship you have with your husband and kids. You have treated them in a certain way since you and your husband were young. In your role as wife and mother, you have established a pattern of behavior through the years. Their needs changed somewhat as they grew older, but your role is still pretty much the same. Your role is to satisfy their needs whatever they may be now. You may be more financially comfortable now, or not. Your kids may be out of the house or still living with you. Your husband may be retired or not. Those different scenarios affect the services required of you, but your role is still the same.

So all the circumstances surrounding you and the particular dynamics of your household don't matter. You can still make a change in your life, and they will adapt. When you get older, your husband needs you more than you need him. Your kids really need you less and less, but they love the convenience you bring into their lives, and they will take advantage of it. You have to get rid of that nurturing feeling. You have to get rid of the guilt and recognize their needs compared to the convenience you provide, and you have to find more purpose to your life than just serving and pleasing everyone else.

Start living life, and they will adjust. Don't be constantly on call for any reason. Now, you can't really go crazy and turn 180 degrees on everyone at once. You can't just stop doing everything and start behaving as if you're entitled because of all the years you've served them. You can't expect them to now serve you in exchange. You need to bring balance to the change. Let them know that you're not going to be there for every call, that there are things you want to do while you're still alive. You have the right to be happy, so things will change. It will be your lifestyle change. You will cut down on your chores and add some "me time" for things you want to do. Hopefully there are things that you still want to do. Hopefully you haven't forgotten what you like after years of caring about everyone else's happiness. But don't worry if you did forget. Just start looking for things you can get involved in. You have to remember that it's a lifestyle change. No one will die if you don't cook every day. No one will get sick if you don't clean every day. They can all do their own laundry and put their clothes away. They can all do lots of chores—they just don't want to. They're not the stupid ones; they know there are better things to do than clean and cook. They won't be happy about pitching in, and they will fight you and complain, but that's too bad. It's your time now. You're not going to get back all those years that you spent putting everyone else ahead of you, so don't waste the ones you have left. If your husband refuses the change stubbornly, you will have to start doing things that you never did before. Learn how to pay bills and balance the checkbook. Take on other responsibilities that will indicate that you're ready to live your life alone if necessary. He will see that you are making changes with or without him in the picture. Perception is everything. You can join the gym or a church group. Take some dancing classes or cooking classes—anything that shows that you want to improve your life. If he wants to sit in front of the TV and wait to die, that's his choice, but you are going to live.

He will complain and challenge you, and he will try to break you down the way he probably did many times before, but this time you stay strong. He can call you a bad wife. He can call you crazy. He can try to get the kids to talk to you and straighten you out. All you have to do is tell them, "I just want to be happy. If you love me you will want me to be happy." So don't let him break you down. The most important thing is to stay strong and not feel guilty.

Remember, your kids don't need you. Just remember what you were doing when you were their age. Remember what you were capable of doing at that stage of your life. You may already have had your own kids when you were their age and had begun your career of taking care of everything. Trust me, they are just as capable as you were; they're just smarter. They are fighting you because they all have more to lose than you do.

Don't be afraid that you will end up alone and that everyone will abandon you. You will still love them, and you'll be there when they really need you, but you have the right to be happy and to enjoy your life doing the things you want to do. Don't wait for anyone else to do it for you. Don't wait for crumbs that someone else will leave for you. Your kids will understand if they love you at all. Your husband will realize how much he needs you and that you will not tolerate his selfish ways anymore. He will compromise because he's got too much to lose if he doesn't. We are all capable of measuring whether it's worth compromising to keep what we love. All you need is to make a decision. Stay strong, and this time they will bend instead of you.

GUIDELINES TO GO BY

CHAPTER 15

You Can Look, But Don't Touch

Now, there's another genius line that men like to use to convince you that it is okay for them to look ... that there is nothing wrong with them looking at other beautiful women. We are not doing anything wrong. You don't know what goes through our minds, so there is no need for you to get pissed off just because we look.

No, you *should* get pissed off. Don't accept that explanation! It's not what we say it is. It never is, and if we can't convince you, we will try really hard to confuse you. Now there are times when a man can notice another nice couple. He can comment on them, see a beautiful woman, maybe admire what she is wearing and suggest that you would look good in it too. That's not what I'm talking about. That man is very open about it. He noticed it, he mentioned it, and he's not hiding it. It's the other silent look that really means, "If you weren't around, I'd be hitting on that." And that does not necessarily meaning you not being around as in him being single. It means if you weren't around at the moment and there was no chance you would find out what he did!

Let me give you an example. You and your husband have a nice dinner at home. You cooked one of his favorite meals. He ate really

– 115 –

well, and now the two of you are going out for some drinks and dancing. When you get to the restaurant or the lounge, would he say, "I want to see what's on the menu. I'm not hungry. I don't want to eat; I just want to look." Has that ever happened? Well if it did, then the rest of this paragraph doesn't apply to you. Here's another example: Has your husband ever gone to the mall "just to see what they have"? Men don't do window-shopping; we don't go shopping if we are not planning to buy something. When we don't buy, it's because we can't afford what we want, or what we want wasn't available. We don't look just to look. We do things with purpose. Our minds work very simply. We are programmed to achieve a goal, to accomplish. We're like Julius Caesar: "Veni, vidi, vici" … I came, I saw, I conquered. So you are very naïve to believe he's "just looking." The reason he's just looking now is the circumstance. Put him in a different city where nobody knows him and you would never find out, and he will be hunting, not looking.

Try an experiment to see how he would like it if you did the same thing. Take a good look at an attractive man and make sure he sees you. If he's doing it, so can you. Perhaps you could say, "I could see myself with a man like that if I wasn't with you." I'm sure he wouldn't like that, and he would try to explain to you that your looking is not the same as his looking. He will try to confuse you if he cannot convince you, but ask him what goes through his mind when he looks at another attractive woman. See what he has to say.

He may try to accuse you of planning to break up with him or preparing yourself just in case it happens. You need to stay strong, and don't apologize. You don't know what he's thinking when he's looking. Don't accept any explanations. They are not true, no matter how much you want to believe him. Maybe he's with you until something better comes along, so why should you be blindsided when his behavior doesn't give you confidence that you two will be together for a very long time.

The jealousy card can bring you a lot of good if you don't overplay it. A man can really love and really be hurt if you leave him, but he would hurt even more if he saw you with someone else. He can live without you, and he will move on, but he will hate to see you with someone else even when the breakup is his own fault, and even if he left you. He will still judge your love for him by how long it takes you to be with someone else. So the jealousy card is a very powerful thing. Just don't hurt his ego to the point of no return. Just the fact that he thinks you are capable of doing something is enough; you don't have to actually do it.

Jealousy and the threat of losing you will keep him attentive to you, because he doesn't want to lose you to another man. He needs to be hunting you so he won't be hunting someone else. So do not be a 100 percent sure thing for him. Don't let him feel that you would never leave him no matter what. There is no challenge there. Bottom line? No looking. No touching.

CHAPTER 16

Relationships are Hard Work

Why do we choose to make our lives harder and get involved in a relationship if it's hard work? Why add to everyday struggles and challenges by being in a relationship if that's what it is—hard work. Is that what you're thinking when you meet someone? When you first start dating, do you hope that it's going to last because you want to work hard on it? That is not how a relationship starts, so why do we simply accept that we have to work hard to keep it? That is not a burden we have in mind when we start planning a future with someone. Why do we accept later on that in order for a relationship to be successful we have to work hard on it?

Imagine choosing a location for your vacation that would offer you a great beach, great food, and awesome entertainment. When you get there, the weather is bad most of the time, or the food is not good, or the entertainment is lame. Now you can put up with this for the few days that you are visiting. You can focus on the good things and deal with the negative aspects for a few days. But what if your lifetime was like this vacation? You would have to work very hard to be happy as you work with the negative elements of life.

Why not just do the work before committing to the vacation? Do some research. Pick a place that offers the highest likelihood that all of your main expectations will be covered. Of course there will be some days when the weather is not good or the food is not up to your standards. That's okay, but vast majority of the experience should be all you want it to be.

The same strategy works with your relationship. Do the hard work when you're picking your mate, and there will be less chance you will have to work all that hard to maintain a happy relationship with him. When you're with someone, you should be in a much better place than you would be in if you were single. Having a partner should make your life better, not harder. That is the life we are all looking for, but the reality is that most people don't get it. When you look at your man twenty to thirty years into your marriage and you say to yourself, *If I met you now and we had no history together—no kids, no memories—and if I were a single woman looking for love and for a life partner, I would pick you because of the way you treat me.* That's how you know you have the right man. Those kinds of relationships are not based on hard work. The couple who has that did not get there by working hard on their relationship. Of course they've had some bad days and some challenges, but never enough of them to question their choice in a partner or to feel as if their love for each other is "work." Those challenges made them stronger as individuals and as a couple, and brought them closer to each other. The challenges did not drive them apart and make each of them blame the other person for any unhappiness. Most couples don't have that; that is not their reality. But you create your own reality, no matter how many of your friends and family members tell you things change when you get married. That is a reflection of their lives, their marriages, and their choices of partners. Their compromises and their understanding of the concept of relationships don't have to be yours.

If you want to work hard on your relationship, that is your choice—and all the best to you. Don't think that the ones who have great relationships are lucky. Don't think it just happened for them ... it was all just luck and had nothing to do with finding their soul mates. Well it wasn't just luck, just as it's not luck that makes most successful business people successful. Most people who are successful in a relationship didn't rely on hope and luck to make it happen. You create your reality. You pick your partner, and if you pick the wrong man you can come up with one hundred excuses to explain why it went wrong, but at the end of the day it's still your life to live. Excuses will not make it easier for you to live with a bad relationship, so don't leave it to chance, and don't leave it to luck.

Take charge. You have the power, and now you also have the knowledge that can help you to pick the right partner.

CHAPTER 17

90 Percent / 10 Percent

Everyone needs some time that we call "me time"; there is nothing wrong with that. When we were kids we had that time. When we were teenagers we had it. Even as a single adult we had that sort of time. We had hobbies and interests, and now that we are married we should still have them.

Yes, things have changed, as we've said. There are more responsibilities when we have a family, and so much less time for anything else. Still, all that doesn't mean that you still can't enjoy the things you enjoyed before. Certain interests you may grow out of, but other interests develop as we grow older. No matter how close you are as a couple, there will always be some hobbies or enjoyable ways of spending time with other people that you will not share with your spouse. You might enjoy spending time with your girlfriends, going for coffee or lunch, maybe doing some shopping or going for a walk—anything just to get out and talk to someone else you can connect with and share different perspectives. Maybe you're a movie buff, and you used to go out with your girlfriends to see the new movies when they came out. You would probably still enjoy that now. If you enjoy reading books, get out of the house, go to the coffee shop, and read while you indulge in your favorite coffee. What are the chances that you will be able to sit down for a couple of hours at home without interruptions? There will always be unanswered questions at home, and the most famous one will be "Are you finished?" Sometimes you may feel guilty sitting down instead of facing that sink full of dishes or that pile of dirty laundry. Once you're in the coffee shop, there is nothing you can do about your chores, and you will be forced to enjoy your peace and quiet. We go to the gym because even working out at home is difficult to schedule and more often than not is interrupted. Once you are out of the house, you can focus on the task or pleasure at hand.

Don't stay home to watch TV or just take a nap. You need to change your daily routine. Indulge in a hobby. Develop interests that are just about you. You need to recharge your batteries and get away from the repetitive routine of job, house, chores, TV, and sleep. Even if you have a great time with your family and your husband, you still need some time away from them.

Your husband will also need some time away from you. Men are usually pretty good at keeping up with the hobbies that will get them out of the house. We do get our "me time" no matter what. Men would also rather stay home and look after the kids for a couple of hours now and then so you can have some time alone. They know that, when you come back, they will see you happy instead of nagging and complaining. Men understand the need to recharge; we have our golf, fishing, and all kinds of sports and hobbies. We enjoy meeting up with the guys, and we'll fight hard to still be able to do it even when we're in a relationship. He should be able to do it, and so should you. It shouldn't be that you each spend most of your free time on different interests, but you should definitely spend some time apart.

Of course, you will have to make that time for yourself by yourself. Nobody will hand it to you. Nobody will say, "Take a few hours for yourself. I'll change my plans and finish your work for you." Yes, I know. If your loved ones loved you and appreciated you, they should say that. But that's not how kids' and husbands' brains are wired. If doesn't mean they don't love you; it just means that they also love what you do for them. So make sure you get some "me time." In the end, everyone will be happier. As I said, keep 10 percent of your time free. A few hours a week … keep it for yourself and only you.

Me, myself, and I …

Chapter 18

Don't Take Out His Fangs

You can get so much out of your man if you do it in the right way. In most cases and in most scenarios men really don't care what happens either way. We let you make choices and many decisions, and we are happy to do it. What we do like is to be considered in the process. If you ask for our opinion, nine out of ten times we will say, "Whatever you like." We may be concerned about the financial cost and how your action makes us look as the man of the house, but that is all there is. All the other concerns we don't really have. The concern over the financial cost I'm sure you understand. The color, texture, and style? We don't care. If you like it, it's good enough for us. The only questions are can we afford it and should we be spending so much on that?

The more you make it look as if we are being appreciated and loved for doing this for you, the more flexible we get. If you make it your right to get what you want because you are an equal provider and you don't have to ask for permission, the more we will fight back, and it's not going to be about the price anymore. Most women don't crave recognition; they don't need the feeling of victory when they get something they want as long as they get it.

You can and should manipulate your man to get what you want. You will get what you want, we will feel like we agreed on it, and everyone will be happy. If you want to get something by getting into a man's face and reading him your rights and your place in the relationship, he will resist you. Even if you're completely right, but you want to get that point across through confrontation, he will resent you and won't forget it. We want to feel like men who provide things for you. We want to be part of you getting what you want. We are emasculated when you say, "I'm getting it, and there's nothing you can do about it." We feel the same effect when you say, "I'm going out with my girlfriends, and I don't need your permission."

We know you don't need our permission, but we won't feel the need to retaliate if you just say, "Honey, if we don't have any plans together for Friday, I'd like to see my girlfriends." This includes your man in a decision that you've probably already made. This is not throwing it in his face. He'll have no problem with your decision.

So, a man will do anything he can for you, but don't try to take his fangs out. Let him feel like a man ... feel like your hero. If you try to get everything you want by making a series of stands, then so will he. The partnership will turn into a competition and a power struggle, and men are usually more ruthless than women. That will not make you or him happy, just more resentful.

CHAPTER 19

Special, Not Essential

As I mentioned before, you want to make your man feel special. Feeling special is a good thing; we all like being around people who make us feel good. We all want to be appreciated and get recognition for the things we do, especially by someone we care about. Remember we men want to be your heroes, and if you don't recognize it and don't acknowledge something we do for you, it won't feel worth the effort.

Again, as I said before, you have to set your standards and demands with your man before he can fulfill them. When he does that, you have to give him recognition. That is the very difference between being a difficult woman and being a woman worth the effort. When you demand certain treatment from your man and you receive it, it is a thing of give and take. You're being treated properly, you're receiving the love and respect from him, and your standards and demands have been met. It's only fair to give it back.

Of course he will also expect certain treatment from you. He expects things in return and a show of appreciation and gratitude for what he has done. The way you handle the good treatment you receive will show the love and respect you have for him. It will make him feel special. It will also show class on your side, and your man will be happy to do things for you. Don't treat his action as if it's not a big deal and it's something men have always done for you, as if it's something that should be done all the time. Even if it is so, don't make yourself look as if you are entitled to it. For whatever reason you may think that you actually are entitled, he will not see it that way. If you feel entitled, you won't think you should give him any special treatment or recognition for what he's done, and that's when you are perceived as demanding and difficult. That's when you become too much effort and not enough reward.

No matter how beautiful or talented or special in any way you are, it will still come down to how you treat each other, and his feelings about himself will be a reflection of the way you treat him. You may have something that he really wants, and he may stick around because of it even if you treat him poorly, but he will not feel obligated to you or feel guilty about something he might be doing behind your back. He will feel no guilt or remorse for disrespecting you, because that's what he's used to getting from you. He can lie to you, cheat on you, or do anything else he wants and simply justify it because of the way you treat him. He will feel that you deserve similar treatment. So, if you're looking to receive good deeds, be ready to give them out.

Now, just as it is important to show your man how special he is, it's also important not to make him feel essential. Don't make him think that no other man has ever treated you as well as he does. Don't make him think that he's the best thing that ever happened to you. He needs to know that your standards are real, and what makes them real is that men always treat you in a way that matches your standards. Any time you were treated any differently, you didn't stick around. You appreciate men who know how to treat a woman ... men who know how to treat a lady and are not threatened by her. On the other hand, you know how to make a man feel special when he's walking hand in hand with you. You have the power to make him feel like a king ... to treat him like the most important person in your life. There are so many great pleasures and life moments you want to share with him, but they all depend on the way he treats you.

He's not entitled to these experiences. He cannot inherit that kind of treatment; he can only earn it. His perfect face or smile or money or great penis won't make a difference ... won't make him special. They only way to get the best out of you is by treating you well.

Chapter 20

The Point of No Return

The point of no return is a difficult time when you realize that there is no going back ... that a relationship is over. You have tried everything you can, everything you know how to do, and you find yourself at the crossroads. Do you stay in a marriage or even a relationship so you won't rock the boat for the sake of everyone else's convenience? Or do you leave? How important is your happiness to you? How important is the rest of your life to you? Have you really tried everything you could? How will your decision be accepted by the people around you—your friends and family? How will this affect everyone's lives. What are you going to do being single? All these questions and more will go through your mind before you take any action. It will feel overwhelming, and it will scare you. You must be at peace with yourself and believe you are making the right decision.

Be prepared. Your husband will fight you; he will be bitter and vengeful. He will call you all sorts of names, try to scare you about being alone, and try to turn everyone against you. In the end, he will even beg and promise that he will change. Keep in mind that his reasons are selfish. He's not worrying about your kids, your friends, or how you will make it on your own. He is thinking only about himself. He doesn't want to let go of what he has, and why would he? You can't really expect him to be supportive and understanding. Your kids might be the same. If they are older, they will worry about losing that home that they can always come back to … a place they can always move back to if they need to. There they will always have you to take care of the grandkids and help them out because you have nothing else to do anyway. They might call you selfish because they don't want to lose what you can do for them. They never have to grow up completely because you are always there to pick up the slack and help out. They might tell you it was your choice to have them and it's your responsibility to help. Expect them to put the guilt trip on, so you might as well put a reverse a guilt trip on them. Tell them that you hoped that your kids would love you the way you love them and not only love the service that your provide for them. Tell them you hoped for kids that would care about your happiness the way you care about theirs and not only think about themselves … kids who would appreciate the years of your life that you put on hold for them, and all the things you did for them. You hoped your kids could care more about your well-being than their own convenience. Guilt trips can always work two ways.

If the kids are younger, they need to know that the dissolution of your marriage has nothing to do with them. Assure them that they will be loved and cared for just as much as before. Divorce isn't taboo anymore, and some of their friends' parents are probably divorced as well, so they won't be in such shock. Talk to them about those friends and see what bothers them about their parents. What issues do their friends have with their parents' divorce? Try to address the issues and assure your children they won't have to face them. Make sure you know what they are worried about so you can anticipate some things that will happen and some questions they will ask you in the future. No one—kids or parents—should be blindsided by anything.

The reactions from your friends and family members will probably range from one extreme to another. Some may say you should have separated a long time ago, and some may try to scare you about your future alone. Your real friends will be there to support you no matter what. Some will be asking for all the little details so they will have something to talk about when they spread gossip. Some will take your husband's side and may not be too nice to you. All of that is fine. None of them can impact your life; you can maintain control. Don't get too disappointed; you might be surprised at who will turn against you. It only means it's time to make new real friends. Hopefully you will make better choices this time. You don't need friends like that. At least the table won't be overcrowded on those few holidays when everyone comes over. It will only be the good friends and family members, and not the ones who judge you if the meal wasn't perfect or the house wasn't freshly vacuumed. Those friends you don't need to care about, because they don't care about you either.

Another thing that will have an impact on your decision to stay or leave is where you live. In smaller communities, your separation will probably be more public than it would be in a big city. Some ethnic and religious groups have bigger issues with divorce than others. It's all in the perception, just as it's the perception of the time we live in. Most women would leave a cheating husband, and most people, especially other women, would say, "Good for you." If he's an alcoholic and never comes home, spends all the money, and she has to raise kids and provide for them on her own, most people would applaud her for leaving. If he's disrespecting her, treating her as a servant, or abusing her verbally, emotionally, or physically— privately or publically—most people would support her decision to leave.

Well, sixty years ago all those things were happening to women more than they are today, but the perception was that there was nothing worse than divorce. I don't know the statistics, but I don't remember any of my grandparent's friends getting divorced. I don't believe that men were so much better to their wives then than they are now. Women just did not leave. They put up with being treated badly. Right now you are looking at the reasons I've mentioned, and you're thinking they justify divorce, but women sixty years ago didn't think so. So who is to say that the reasons for divorce that you have now will not be looked upon as justifiable sixty or thirty or ten years from now? The reasons may not look that bad right now, but that's because women are still willing to sacrifice themselves for others for little in return. Every generation of women has had different obstacles to overcome, and the rights and standards experienced by women in today's society have been built on the backs of women who fought for them … on the backs of the women who realized they should be equal partners in life with their mates.

Life is not a movie in which a man has a leading role and women are there just to support him. No, their roles are just as important, because without them the movie cannot be made. So if you can't make a movie without the woman, she must be just as important as the man. Every positive change that has been made in the lives of women over the years has been made because women fought for it once they realized how important they are.

These changes didn't happen because a bunch of men sat at a table and decided that women should have all the rights so they could challenge men when they were wrong, and they could demand better treatment. A bunch of men didn't decide to give up all the privileges they had in the world because out of the blue their combined conscience told them that their dominance wasn't fair to women.

The women who made the changes were not considered model wives and mothers. They were criticized by men and even other women who didn't want to rock the boat. These women did not care about the perceptions that were in place during their lifetimes. They didn't care about the roles that women had been trained to play since they were little girls. They were driven by their belief in what was right and what was wrong. They didn't doubt themselves and ask their friends and families to support them. Not many had fathers and husbands who told them how proud they were of them. These women weren't afraid to be alone.

Being alone seems to be a more difficult obstacle for a woman than it is for a man. To a man it's simple fact: he'd rather be alone or be free than be someone's servant. For a woman, being alone seems to be an obstacle to overcome. If you can shake off that nurturing feeling—the feeling of nesting and taking care of everyone—as well as the infatuation with being in a relationship, you will be better off alone than in an unhappy marriage. There are so many things that you can do for yourself that will give you purpose for existence, a feeling of accomplishment, and an all-around good feeling about yourself. You can study yoga, go back to school, start a career. You can improve your physical as well as your mental and intellectual well-being. It doesn't matter what you choose; what matters is that you will interact with other people who have similar interests and who pursue them for the same reasons you do. These are people with whom you will have things in common, and that's how your circle of friends will expand. You will meet people who want to explore new horizons instead of sitting around gossiping about someone else's life. You can start to travel and expand your understanding of the world beyond the views of the people you've hung out with all your life.

Most importantly, take care of number one—you. If you have the need to help and nurture, there are so many organizations that could use a good-hearted volunteer like you. There are programs through which you can help the unfortunate. You can help children who need you much more than the twenty-five-year-old you have at home needs you. You can help with animal care; you can help with fundraising for all kinds of well-meaning organizations. Get involved in your community—those people who really need help know how to sincerely appreciate someone like you. Nothing can beat that feeling.

Being alone is not sitting alone in an empty apartment waiting to die. Being alone means being free to pursue your dreams and fulfill your needs … to meet new people, indulge in new experiences, and take care of number one.

Being alone shouldn't scare you and hold you back. Remember the most important thing: you have the power. It's your life to live. Will you make a change or will you come to the end of your life full of regrets and excuses? Either way, it is still your life to live.

CHAPTER 21

Guidelines

Remember these important guidelines:

- You have the power.
- Be approachable.
- Set your standards.
- Be ready to walk away.
- Date more than one person.
- Be a bus, not a taxi.
- Everything a man can do, you can do better.
- Don't nag (actions speak louder than words).
- If he's not chasing you, he's chasing someone else.
- Men need women more than women need men.

I have created this quiz for Halloween parties with some good friends of mine. It may not be for everyone, but I'm sure that some of you will enjoy it. It's always a good way to finish your day with a laugh, even if you're laughing at yourself. There are five questions for men and five questions for women. Both parties should answer both sets of questions and then compare answers out loud. You must choose from the available answers.

Questions for Men:

1. If you had one wish what would it be?

    a. I want to go back in time before I met her and change everything.
    b. I want her to get into shape, put out more, and talk less.
    c. I want $20 million and divorce.

2. What was your mother's comment after she met her for the first time?

    a. I guess you did the best you could.
    b. Now I know there really is another mother more disappointed than I am.
    c. Another one of those, like you sister isn't enough?

3. What did you think the first time you had sex?

    a. No pot of gold at the end of this rainbow.
    b. Compared to what I had before, this is not so bad.
    c. Oh my God! And I thought her cousin was good.

4. Describe your wife as a lover

    a. She's somewhat participating.
    b. She's pretty good when she stays awake.
    c. The better she is, the longer the "honey do" list becomes.

5. If she died, to show your respect, for the first six months you would:

    a. Wear only a black condom.
    b. Sleep only with women who knew her so you could share stories later.
    c. Open up a massage parlor and name it after her.

Questions for Women: ▨▨▨▨▨▨▨▨▨▨▨▨▨▨

1. What's the first thing your girlfriends thought after they met him?

    a.   Well, let's hope he's got money.
    b.   Typical prom queen story: the higher you fly, the lower you fall.
    c.   I hope he's gotten better since I was with him the last time.

2. What did you think after sex for the first time?

    a.   Finally done and over with.
    b.   Took me longer to take my clothes off than it did to have sex.
    c.   Oh my God! He really is bigger than any of his friends.

3. When you first found out you were pregnant, your thoughts were:

    a.   All right! This will get me out of sex for the next nine months.
    b.   I hope it doesn't look like him.
    c.   God, I hope it's his!

4. If your hubby was in a coma and was being looked after by a very handsome male nurse you would:

    a.   Blindfold him just in case he woke up.
    b.   Pull the plug so it wouldn't be considered cheating.
    c.   Push him off the bed and give yourself some more room.

5. If there was an earthquake while you were in bed with your hubby, you would:

    a.   Pull him on top in case the ceiling comes down.
    b.   Run out and let the firemen pull him out.
    c.   Save the kids and starting looking for a younger model of him.